Small Steps

to

Bigger Book Sales

Glenn Ashton B.A., LL.B., M.B.A.

https://www.amazon.com/author/glennashton
Email: smallsp@telus.net

Small Steps to Bigger Book Sales

Disclaimer and terms of use agreement:

Dedication to Rebel writers

This book is dedicated to all writers who wish to self-publish their own books through Amazon and Kindle, and to promote them.

You are a Rebel, about to join the worldwide *Gutenberg+ Revolution* that Amazon and Kindle have made possible.

No longer will writers be dependent upon the whims of traditional publishers. We now have the keys to our very own printing presses (the high speed ones of Amazon, and the virtual ones of Kindle). Just as Gutenberg in the 1450's set the world free by inventing the first printing press, so too are we now all free to print and promote our very own books. Welcome to the Revolution!

If are not yet a writer, but want to greatly improve your social networking skills (your use of Facebook, Google+, Twitter, your blog, Pinterest etc.), then you will find many ideas in this book.

https://www.amazon.com/author/glennashton

Please email me about your own journey using your *Small Steps Plan*, at smallsp@telus.net

Acknowledgments

This book is based on my earlier book, **Your Purrfect Way to Publish & Promote Your Amazon & Kindle Books**. *Your Purrfect Way* is available as both Amazon print on demand, and as an eBook on Kindle.

Your Purrfect Way is a 461-page reference work for those who want to learn how to publish and promote their own books.

This book is a shorter summary of the main steps you can take to market your own books, and is revised to make it easier to read, and updated. It is also useful for anyone wishing to improve their use of social media (their use of Facebook, blogging, Twitter, forums etc.)

So as to keep *The Small Steps* short and easy to read, but still very useful, I have not included some of those *Your Purrfect Way* hyperlink references in it.

Table of Contents

1   What this Book will do for You

You will be guided to do 20 Tasks, as part of your very own **Small Steps Plan** to market your books.

You will start with the first 10 tasks over 3 months and the next 10 over the next 6 months. Then you review and revise your next Small Steps Plan.

You will prepare a book promotion plan that will show you how to take methodical, small steps every week to market your books where they stand the best chance of being bought by readers.

You will learn how to:

- create your *Dream Team* of advisors to help you every step of the way;
- define your *Target Readers,* so that you can fashion hooks to persuade them to buy your books;
- find and use many of top social network *forums*, where readers and writers mix, so that you can build your own team of supporters, your very own friendship group or *Clan*;
- get *reviews* of your books;
- use other *social networks* tools easily and effectively; and do all this at your own speed and in the free time you have.

In Chapter 25 you have a *template* for your own **Small Steps Plan**, designed to make it easy for your to prepare your first plan. Chapter 26 has a very detailed 120-item **Weekly Engagement Checklist**.

Your Small Steps Plan will help you build a solid Author Platform, which is the base for all your future book marketing efforts.

Think of your Author Platform as taking the shape of a home, as in the diagram below.

YOUR AUTHOR PLATFORM HOME

Twitter Plan

Furniture:
Social Networks
(including Google+, Pinterest, LinkedIn, Goodreads, Shelfari, Digg, Reddit, Stumbleupon, Delicious, Squidoo, AuthorsDen, Nexopia, Triberr, Blog Nation, Weread)

3rd floor: *Email Plan*

Furniture:
Forums, Book reviews, Author videos, Blog Talk Radio

2nd floor: *Facebook Page*

Furniture:
Amazon & Kindle Promotion

1st Floor: *Author Blog*

The Foundation:
Author Brand, Dream Team of advisors, Target Readers and Promotion Plan

3 The Small Steps, Small Wins Strategy

This is a strategy that has been proven to work and has helped millions of people to carry out their plans.

You will start with three big, important chunks of work, which you will break down into smaller bits that allow you to get them done easily and fast. The three big jobs are to define your own Author Brand, then to set up your own Dream Team of Advisors, and then to work with your Team to define your Target Readers.

The Big 3

Your ***Author Brand*** should tell the market what you and your products (your books) have to offer. <u>You want your Brand to be unique, different, special, outstanding, and pleasurable</u>.

Wikipedia has this definition of a Brand: A name, term, design, symbol, or any other feature that identifies one seller's good or service as distinct from those of other sellers.

What is your ***Dream Team of Advisors***?

Your Dream Team is your very own personally picked team of advisors.

We will talk about how you go about choosing the number you need, the types of people you need, what you want them to do to help you promote your books, and how to invite them to join your Team.

Your aim is for your Dream Team to be there for you at each stage of your Promotion Plan, helping you in your experiments, acting as a sounding board, adding value, and keeping your spirits up.

Many successful people have used this method on their road to success (Jack Canfield of *Chicken Soup for the Soul* is a firm believer in having a personal coach to help you clarify your goals and support you when you need support; Napoleon Hill of *Think and Grow Rich* and *The Law of Success* fame favored a mastermind group as a means to success in business).

How do you define your **Target Readers**?

The Small Steps Plan gives you solid ideas about how to do this.

You are looking to find a tiny niche, and to carve it out from all the millions of book buyers worldwide. That's what 'Target Readers' or target markets means to you. <u>Your very own niche readers.</u>

Your aim is to form a core of readers whose interest in and purchase of your book will act as yeast – leading to more readers from other groups.

John Locke – the man who sold a million eBooks – writes that every action you take must have just one aim: to find your target audience, to write to them, and to convert them into what he calls guaranteed buyers of your coming books.

More about Small Steps and Small Wins

The Small Steps & Small Wins strategy is very effective because it makes the planning process much simpler, and motivates people to achieve the targets they set themselves. Your Small Steps Plan will be built around a series of concrete, complete outcomes of moderate importance to ensure that you build a pattern of successes.

The concept of **Small Wins** comes from a book called *Enterprise* by Gartner and Bellamy. According to the authors, *Small Wins are achievable, tangible accomplishments that are within a person's capabilities and can produce a visible result.*

So a small win:

- Is an outcome of "moderate importance".
- Does not have to be the logical next step towards your goal – it can be out of the logical order of steps.
- It moves you towards your goal but not necessarily in a straight line.
- Is a "win" that preserves the gains you got from other small wins – so small wins reinforce each other's gains.

So "small" does not mean insignificant. It is "small" because you are more likely to achieve it than to fail to achieve it.

TIP: Make your mountains small, and you can climb them more easily.

The Small Steps, Small Wins strategy has a sound psychological base. You pile up small wins, accumulate gains, and make it easier to continue towards your goals.

The Small Step Plan is based on achieving **clear goals** so that you know what you are working toward. The clearer your goals, the easier it is to decide on small steps to achieve them, and the more small wins you have towards that goal, the more you will start believing in your own ability to reach your goals.

Your *Small Steps Plan* will show you how to set clear goals.

The 120-point **Weekly Engagement Checklist** in Chapter 26 is designed to make it easy for you to reviews each week your progress and planning for intensive, effective interaction on the social networks you will use to market your small tasks you included in your *Small Steps Plan.*

Note that in the ***Small Steps Plan template*** in Chapter 25, the tasks to be done by you and included in your first such Plan are broken down into two bins of work. Bin 1 contains Tasks numbers 1 to 10 (dealt with in chapters 5 to 14), while Bin 2 contains Tasks numbers 11 to 20 (see chapters 15 to 24).

TIP: My suggestion is that you get your Plan up and running by first putting into that Plan only the Bin 1 tasks. Once you have started implementing those tasks, you can include Bin 2 tasks.

TIP: Using the 120-point ***Weekly Engagement Checklist*** in Chapter 26 each week with your Team will allow you easily to check your planning and progress, without fearing that you have missed something.

If at any time you feel overwhelmed, consider moving a task from Bin 1 to Bin 2 (other than the Big 3: setting up your Dream Team, defining your Author Brand, and defining your Target Readers).

You can also work on another task in Bin 1 and come back later on to the one that is causing you grief.

More information for you:

If you want to explore any task in more detail than as discussed in this book, just Google the task topic and scan some of the website posts that you are shown.

5   Task 1: Your Dream Team of Advisors

1   Introduction:

Your Dream Team is your handpicked team of personal coaches or Mastermind group.

You want your Team to be there for you at every stage of your Small Steps Plan, helping you in your experiments, acting as a sounding board, adding value, and keeping your spirits up.

2   How many Team members?

Choose members from your relatives and friends, to start with.

They will form your local ***Dream Team***.

They are the team that is close enough to talk to personally, if you have to.

Later on, you can form another complementary team, your online or Clan, selected from your Clan or tribe (see Task 15).

TIP: Keep your local Dream Team small to start with – I suggest 3 to 5 members.

You can have many more members in your online Clan Dream Team (where the interaction will be less frequent and less intensive).

If you cannot think of enough members to ask, then ask your relatives and friends for suggestions.

If you ask someone to join, and they agree, then ask them for suggestions for other members.

3   **What kind of people?**

The most important thing is that you are comfortable with your Dream Team members.

Think about the contents of your Plan. Do you know anybody with experience or skills in some of the areas in the Plan?

4   **How often to meet?**

You will need to talk to them about how often, and how, you meet – physically and/or via email or by telephone or Skype. Start with once every two weeks – later on, say after 3 months, you can make it once a month.

Of course, between meetings you and your Team will be talking to each other about all the things that crop up when you are putting together a business plan, and taking steps under the plan.

5   **Preparation before meeting:**

As a first step, I suggest that you make a gift to any prospective member of your Team of the Amazon printed version of this book (***Small Steps to Bigger Book Sales***). This will help you all sing off the same hymn book, and will be very useful an agenda for your discussions with Team members. It will help them decide if they wish to help you and join your Team.

6   **What will your Team will be doing?**

Your Team will help you draw up your Small Steps Plan, and settle on your Author Brand.

In particular, your Team will help you with these:

Target Readers: Deciding who your target markets (Target Readers) are, and fleshing out Personas to represent each niche market (see Task 3).

Messages testing: Testing each promotion message (Tweet, Facebook entry, author blog post, emails etc.) you prepare against each of your Target Reader Personas to make sure they are consistent and appropriate for each Persona Family member – including role playing.

7   Your *Editorial Content Plan*:

You should start a short list of topics you plan to cover, over the next 6 months or so, in your various messages to your Target Readers.

Keep it simple, keep it short, and keep it flexible.

Don't sweat the details too much; just jot down broad themes of things you and your Team think might interest your Target Readers.

Your Editorial Content Plan sets the **overall goals** for the type of content of the many messages you will use; it is the overall plan that decides the aims of, the content of, and the date you will send, your many messages.

8   Kick starting your Clan:

Consider having your Dream Team invite their relatives and friends to join your Community as Clan members, so as to kick start your tribe (see Task 3).

1 Branding: With you or without you

Never forget this: You have a choice. You can proactively create and maintain your own Author Brand, or your readers and others will do it for you.

If others do it, you do not control the quality or content of the Author Brand, nor its consistency.

But *you will be branded* – every message from you, every social network channel you use, will contribute to your brand in the minds of the readers (positively or negatively or neutrally).

This means you have to actively manage your Brand, not just leave it to chance or to others.

2 What is an Author Brand?

An Author's Brand means that image which people have in their minds and associate with you as a writer.

It's a mental picture that comes to mind when readers think of any author.

If you want another way of putting it, your brand is what resonates with readers when they see or hear your name. Think John le Carre and Spies. That's branding. Think Ian Fleming and James Bond: an author brand and a product brand, linked forever.

3 How do you create an Author Brand?

You build an Author Brand.

You work on the image, the resonance that you want people to see and hear when your name comes up. You have to give yourself, as a writer, a personality that you want your readers to associate with you.

How do you create that personality?

You aim all your **brand touches** (that is, your interactions with readers, such as your Facebook Page, your Author Blog, your Twitter messages, your book title, cover, content, all images of you or your book) at this author personality.

You are trying to guide the reader to think of your personality traits: so come up with a handful of traits to fit the personality of you as author.

See this article by Lowell entitled *Branding: The Mechanics of Branding*, for more tips on personality traits:
http://www.activegarage.com/branding-the-mechanics-of-branding

This is from Lowell's article:

"You should have 4-6 traits (5 is ideal), each being a single term, usually an adjective.
Authentic, Creative, Innovative, Approachable
Trustworthy, Trendy, Cool, Desirable, Reliable
Relevant, Honest, Flexible, Unique, Relevant
How you define the personality determines the tone and voice of your brand, and therefore all your communications. A brand that is "hip, cool, trendy" sounds decidedly different from one that is "honest, trustworthy, reliable"."

Now brainstorm with your Team about what author brand fits you and your writing, and what types of words and actual words would fit this author brand of yours.

Do you share some with your competitors? Why and what?

4   Mind Mapping your Author Brand:

One way to start the Author Brand brainstorming session with your Team is to use the concept known as *Mind Mapping*.

A mind map is a diagram that you draw using circles and words to reflect your thoughts about something.

How to you use a Mind Map?

You write a key word or key concept right slap in the middle of a sheet of paper, and draw a circle around it. Put your name there. Or a word that you think describes your book's genre. Or a word that you think you would like to represent one of the words that spring to mind when people think of your Author Brand. Or use all of these words to see what the results are.

Then you jot down around this central circle any words that come to mind when you think of the central word or concept. Draw a circle around each one, and link it with a line to the central circle.

If a new word gives birth to another word, write that down, draw a circle and a link back to the second word. Soon you will have several circles, some branching off from others, but all traceable back to the central word.

Have each of your Dream Team do the same with you in mind, and then compare them and talk about them.

5   Emotional Resonance of your Brand:

Your aim is a set of words or images or concepts in your reader's mind which have emotional resonance with that reader, and which spring to mind when they hear or see your name or your book.

The **emotional resonance** is important – your Author Brand will be pretty bland if all the words your readers think of lack any emotional connection to them, and are boring and flat and cardboardish. Why would they take the risk to buy your book if that is what your Author Brand is to them?

6   Your Author Branding Story:

Build your Author Brand on a story about you (your **Author Branding Story**). Make sure the story is in your social network channels: in your author biography on Amazon, in your Amazon Author Page.

Your Author Brand should be authentic and have substance.

Your foundational story on which your Author Brand is built should tell your readers about your Journey on the path to becoming a writer. Who and what influenced you? What values drive you? What makes you different from other writers, makes you unique: why should someone want to read your books?

Drill down deeply to your very core and focus. *You want compelling, unique, focused images and words for your very own Brand Identity.*

Write it in the first person to see how that resonates with you and your Dream Team.

7   Your Author Story & Target Readers:

How does your Author Branding story link to, intertwine with, travel along with, impact that of your various Target Reader Personas (see Task 3)?

Does it compel them? Why?

What links do your Team see between you and your Personas?

If *you* cannot see any emotional links between your Author Brand story and your Target Reader Personas, why should they? And without some emotional link, why should they see you as anything more than yet another boring cardboard writer?

Joanna Penn has a good 2012 article on Author Branding entitled *Branding for Writers: An Essential Step to Building Your Author Platform*:

http://www.thecreativepenn.com/2012/03/20/brandi ng-author-platform/

To Joanna Penn branding is about communication; the ability to connect your purpose as a writer with that of your target readers.

8   Your Author Brand Elevator Speech:

Every writer needs a ***Book Elevator Speech*** to describe her book. The purpose of your elevator speech is to hook the listener by describing your book in very few words, in a way that makes them want to read it. It is called an elevator speech because you are forced to write a speech that can be told to a possible publisher when he gets on the elevator on the tenth floor with you.

You have to hook him before the elevator reaches the ground.

Your speech has to let him know the genre of your book, your possible target market readers, and what the book is about.

Why do you need an elevator speech? You need it because it forces you to penetrate the heart of your book and describe its essence, but in a way that hooks the listener and makes her want more.

In the same way, you need an ***Author Brand Elevator Speech***.

Now brainstorm with your Team about an Elevator Speech describing your Author Brand.

When that person leaves that elevator 30 seconds later, will you – your brand – linger in their mind for days, and compel them to do something about it (such as buy and read your book)?

Practice your ***Author Brand Elevator Speech*** on others – friends, relatives, strangers – to see how it goes over.

When you have a good one, think about how to include it in your author descriptions in all your social network channels.

Make sure your Author Brand is easy to remember, and striking.

Is there passion in your brand? If not, go back to the drawing board. You need passion to move people, to make an emotional link that lingers.

9   What is your Author Brand's promise?

Laura Lowell writes about the promise implicit in Author Brands:

http://www.activegarage.com/branding-whats-your-brand-promise

She writes that only once you understand what your brand promises to your readers can you begin to prioritize your strategies and define your tactics around that brand.

Think about that: What promise do you want your Author Brand to make to possible readers and buyers of your book?

And does your book deliver on that promise?

If part of my Author Brand was this: *Glenn Ashton writes interesting books,* what does this mean for my books?

Branding = Promise.

From you to your readers.

And your delivery on that promise leads to heightened **Brand Trust** in your readers. And this higher level of Brand Trust is what helps your *readers* to convert themselves into *followers* who want to read everything you have written – into repeat buyers. To become what John Locke calls Guaranteed Buyers.

And it turns them into your *Brand Ambassadors* (see Task 4).

10   Elements of your Author Brand:

The elements of your Author Brand consist of all the items covered by your Author Platform Home.

Each part of your Home channels should immediately and clearly project your chosen Author Brand.

So your brand elements include:

- Your name (blog, Facebook, pen name);
- your images (cover, author photo, other);
- your keywords;
- your Author Brand Elevator Speech;
- your Book Elevator Speech;
- your Author biography;
- your book description;

- your book categories;
- the colors of your book's cover and your blog;
- your messages (tweets, blog posts, Facebook posts).

11   Is your Author Brand working?

The ultimate test: Is your book selling?

Other tests of Brand effectiveness are:

- if you are being Followed on Twitter (Task 10), being retweeted in response to your "please Re-tweet" added to each of your Tweets, and Mentioned;
- if your book is being Tagged on Amazon;
- if your Facebook Likes have increased (see Task 6);
- if your participation in the Forums you chose is steady and satisfactory (see Task 7 and Task 14);
- if your emails are being replied to (see Task 11);
- if the membership in your Clan is increasing (see Task 4);
- if any Target Readers have become your Brand Ambassador and are spreading the word (see Task 4); and
- if the goals you set for each of your social network channels are being met.

Now go forth and brand yourself!

1 Introduction:

In this part we deal with these important matters:

- What is a Target Market for an author?
- Who are the Power Readers (the biggest buyers) and how does that influence your choice of target markets?
- What is a Persona, and how can this concept help you better define your very own Target Readers?
- How can you and your Team best define Personas to help you tailor your messages to your Target Readers?

2 What is a Target Market for an Author?

You are looking to find *a tiny niche*, and carve it out from all the millions of book buyers worldwide. That's what 'Target Markets' means to you. <u>Your very own niche readers</u>.

Once you have narrowed your target markets (= Target Readers) down into the smallest niches you can, you start to think of designing the Hooks you need for each such niche, to grab their attention.

This article *Guide to Targeting Your Audience* by Maria Murnane gives you some ideas on how to define your target markets:

<u>https://www.createspace.com/en/community/docs/D</u>
<u>OC-1553</u>

She has ideas on how to identify your audience, understand your audience and target your audience.

One way to approach defining your Target Readers is to start by considering just who are the frequent buyers of eBooks - that is, Power Readers.

3   What are eBook Power Buyers?

Digital Book World surveyed eBook readers in 2011 to get a handle on who the power buyers of eBooks (frequent buyers) were, who influenced them etc. The results can be found in an article headed *Digital Book World 2011: Who Buys E-books, How Many, and Why?* here:

http://style-matters.com/blog/digital-book-world-2011.html

When you read these results, ask yourself whether you think your eBook readers might fit into the same categories as the majority of eBook readers shown in the DBW survey do.

If you think your readers won't, then what does this mean for your promotion campaigns?

4   Free Books as a great Hook:

Now for something else you can use: a whopping 40% of power buyers bought an eBook after receiving a free sample chapter. And 30% bought an eBook after getting another free eBook from the same author. **So free samples and free eBooks do tempt readers to buy eBooks.** How does that fit into your promotion Plan?

5   A Power Buyer Persona for you?

In another study of Power Buyers of eBooks in 2011, the Book Industry Study Group (the U.S. book industry's trade association for policy, standards and research) defined her this way:

She is 44 years old; she loves romance; she spends more buying books now than she did in the past; and she buys at least one eBook a week.

Power Buyers like her represent less than one in five eBook readers, but they buy more than 60% of all eBooks sold; and *the most influential influences on the decision to buy eBooks are free samples and low prices.*

So, should one of your own Target Reader Personas be **Power Buyer Penny**, modelled on the above result?

6   Creating Target Reader Personas:

This is a marketing method which helps teams of designers of products to focus on the needs and wishes of potential purchasers, with greater clarity and a common concept of just who the customer is.

Dip into this site for more on how to create a persona:

http://www.dummies.com/how-to/content/create-a-persona-to-identify-who-your-online-custo.html

7   What is a Persona?

A persona is a snapshot of your potential book buyers.

You create your personas by creating a profile of the demographics of your Target Readers. A Persona is a reader archetype.

8   How many Personas do you need?

I suggest that you start with just 4 Personas, and build up to more as you get more comfortable with defining your Target Readers.

9   Your 5th Persona, Rebecca Random:

I suggest you add to your list of 4 Personas one more: I call her *Rebecca Random*.

Leonard Mlodinow points out in *The Drunkard's Walk* that we often have very little control over our lives and events, and that much of what happens is a 'drunkard's walk', which is something that moves in a random and unpredictable manner.

So we hedge our bets, and add Rebecca Random to our list of Personas.

And 20% of your marketing efforts should be devoted to devising messages that appeal to Rebecca Random. Why? Just in case your 4 Personas don't really capture the most important reader segments you should be targeting.

10   Who is Rebecca Random?

She represents the gods of chance. She represents all those others out there who do not fall under your chosen 4 Personas.

These are her vital statistics, which you experiment with on a random basis by changing them often when writing your social network messages:

Gender –

She is female, because around 68% of readers are female. But, just in case, every now and then – say, in about 10% of the cases – you and your Team should think of her as being a male, with a quick name change to *Robert Random.*

Age –

She is anything between 7 years old, and 85 years old, and at any given time she could be anywhere on that range.

26

Education –

Her educational background is a random range: from no high school to a Ph.D. in nuclear science.

Interests –

Randomly eclectic; in a word, just about everything you could think of.

Personality –

Is she stable? No; think of her as being, at best, quirky and unpredictable.

Fun –

And Rebecca Random represents Fun.

What does that mean?

That you must spend a bit of your messaging on topics that are just pure fun. You have fun in being a bit zany in what you use and how you use it, just in case your seriously chosen, Team discussed, 4 Personas miss out on a big slice of humanity who might love to buy your book and then line up for the next 10 in your series.

Try a little bit of anything. What's the downside? You have fun. Your imagination is stimulated. Your blog posts and forum comments have a small portion (the 20%) that are off the wall. You have a great story to talk about in your blogs describing your journey as an Indie. And you have placed a bet on the drunkard's walk theory being true.

So welcome to Rebecca Random, and treat her well. She might surprise you!

11   How do you build a Persona?

Once you have a sense of just who the Target Readers are for your book(s), then you focus on them, and make them come alive *by thinking of them as actual people.*

Write a brief description of each Persona you and your Team have chosen.

12 Ask your readers to help:

Ask your readers to Help Make My Personas Better. You need information *about them* so that you can improve your Personas.

Find out their ages, their gender, the economic groupings, the family size, education, likes and dislikes, skill sets, wishes and hopes, goals and aspirations, reasons for buying books, what is important for them and why. Where do they hang out online? Who would they listen to when it comes to deciding to buy a book?

Then use this information in improving your Personas.

13 Make them real:

Aim at making your Personas fully fledged individuals, with their own personalities, skills, histories, backgrounds, emotions, wishes. They should be more than simple cardboard characters. *Give them names and ages.*

Make then real; make them compelling. Give them their personal stories. If it helps, clip out a photo of each Persona so that you and your Team can visualize him or her when you talk about the messages.

14 How to start creating Personas:

Three steps:

- you start on your own;
- then you brainstorm them with your Team;
- then you share them with your Readers.

Take a quick stab at creating your Personas on your own and then share them with your *Team.* Your quick definition will help kick start your brainstorming with your Team.

Ask yourselves what rings true about your Personas? What needs changing? Are they alive enough? Is the detail you put into them enough to fashion your messages to appeal to them?

And then share your Personas with your Target Readers and ask them to comment on the Family. Are people missing? Do they ring true? Do they see themselves in them?

15   More on Personas:

Check these sites for more on Personas:

http://www.wqusability.com/articles/personas_storytelling.html

http://www.smartinsights.com/marketplace-analysis/customer-analysis/web-design-personas/

The first site, with the article Personas and Storytelling, gives an example of how one could build a Persona from demographic information by adding specifics and context to the Persona you are building.

The second site, by David Chaffey (*An introduction to using personas to create more customer-centric websites*) gives some examples of Personas for a website.

Dip into Heidi Cohen's *12 Point Marketing Persona Checklist* for more ideas about how to flesh out your own Personas:

http://heidicohen.com/marketing-persona/

The dummies.com site has an interesting article on how to create a Persona to identify who your online customers are, found here:

http://www.dummies.com/how-to/content/create-a-persona-to-identify-who-your-online-custo.html

The writer says keep in mind your personas represent behavior patterns, not job descriptions. The persona should give a well-rounded picture of attitudes, skills and goals. You should group this information in ways that give the most complete picture of the person. Do not model personas after people you know because this can distort the way you feel about them.

16   Use One Primary Persona in the Family:

It might help to have one **Primary Persona** in your Family of Personas.

That Persona will be a bit more broadly fleshed out than the more detailed individual ones, to let you work with the broader appeal of your book.

If you want some quick and dirty testing for a promotional message, use the Primary Persona.

You could start with one Primary Persona and graduate to the Family once you and your Team have played with the use of Personas and are comfortable with the concept.

17   How to Use your Personas:

You and your *Team* use your Target Reader Personas to test each and every message you send to your potential readers as part of your Small Steps Plan.

It is a means to impose *discipline* on yourself when you plan and draw up your promotional campaigns, and send out your messages, but to do so in a way that is *fun* for you and your Team.

See if your message fits their needs, wishes, wants, likes, dislikes, personality.

Don't forget that 20% or so of your messages must be aimed at hooking **Rebecca Random**! And what about **Power Buyer Penny**? Also just in case.

18   Role-Playing and Your Personas:
Do some *role-playing* with your Team if this works for you and them.

19   Talk to your Personas:
Take each Persona in turn, and address them by name; ask them what they think about your planned message or promotional campaign. Is the level of your communication in your message just right to get their attention and hold their attention – are you speaking his or her language? What about the style and tone of your message? Would it convert them into followers? Is your message to that Persona authentic, or does it seem false or contrived?

Tailor your content strategy to each Persona Family member.

20   Ask your Readers to Help:
Use your blog, email, Twitter and other social network channels to invite your readers to participate in a survey to help you refine your Target Readers Personas. Check the article by Steve Baty entitled *User Research for Personas and Other Audience Models* for some hints (Google it).

21   Use Surveys to find your Lost Tribe:
Surveys will cost you nothing (using free programs) except your time to set them up and an analyze any replies you get, and are very flexible.

You can decide in your Small Steps Plan on a range of topics you want to research with your readers, using surveys to find out who they are and what they think, and then work your way through the topics with *each* survey geared to *one* of those topics. This reduces your work, keeps your research very focused, and lets you coordinate your survey topic with your social network messages of the day. Ask them for hints about how you can find what one writer referred to as "your lost tribes" (those you have not yet contacted or have not joined your Clan).

You can then use this information to design your messages (blog posts etc.) to each of your Personas.

22 Consider Joint Surveys:

Check with other members of the Indie Community and/or your writers club, if you have one, whether they want to use similar surveys, and you can then pool the results and learn from each other. Ask readers who they think buys different genres of books.

23 Nitty-Gritty definitions of your Personas:

Here are some points you and your Team need to consider when trying to define your Target Readers Personas:

a. *Phrases* –
Define them with several phrases, not just one or two.

b. *Chunking* –
Drill down in your definitions, so that you are not using definitions which are so general that just about everybody qualifies. Break them

down into smaller chunks or groups, and then into still smaller ones.

c. **Gender –**

Do your books appeal to males more than females, or to both equally (which is unlikely)? Women buy just under 7 out of 10 of all books sold.

d. **Ages –**

Do your books appeal to children? To young adults? To young men and women? To middle-aged readers? To older readers? Why?

e. **Words –**

What type of words would you use to communicate with these groups of Target Readers? Match your own language in your promotion to your Targets.

f. **Income –**

How much do your Target Readers earn – low, medium or high earners?

g. **Education –**

Are your groups of Target Readers school dropouts? Finished school? College educated? Higher educated than that?

h. **Numbers –**

Are there lots of people in your various groups of Target Markets? Or are there very few?

i. **Location –**

Geographically, where would most of those Target Market segments live? Which countries? Which parts of those countries?

j. **Influencers –**

This is a key question.

Who might influence the decision of your groups of Target Markets to buy your book?

For example, if you wrote a children's book, influencers (or actual buyers) might include parents, siblings, grandparents, relatives, teachers, librarians, church volunteers etc.

Ask yourself who influences your purchases of books, to kick start this inquiry.

Often, these purchasing influencers become Target Markets themselves, but your promotion messages might have to be altered for them. Influencers include reviewers of books.

k. *Competition* –

Think of the books of your competitors. Who do they appeal to? Who might their Target Readers be? How does this help you to refine your definitions of your own Target Readers?

l. *Needs* –

A key question.

Just what needs of your Target Markets do or should your books meet?

Emotional needs? Vocational needs? Entertainment needs? Occupational needs? Self-esteem needs? Other needs?

How do potential readers benefit from my book?

Just why would a reader buy my book? What's in it for them? Why do you and your Dream Team buy certain books?

Do some brainstorming with your Team on how you might tell your Target Readers that your book meets their needs.

m. *Seasonal* –

Is there a definite season for selling your book? Why? How can you wrap your promotion around this?

n. *Social media* –

Do the groups use Twitter? Facebook? Forums? Blogs? Follow blogs? How and why?

o. *Amazon & Kindle Forums* –

Which types of Amazon and Kindle forums would each group of Target Markets participate in, if any? Any other types of Forums?

p. *Genre* –

What hints does your book's genre give you about who possible readers and buyers might be?

q. *Other Books* –

What else will your Target Reader be reading? Any hints for your promotion campaign from this?

r. *Feedback* –

Ask readers of your Author Blog and Facebook Page to let you know who they think your Target Markets for your book(s) should be.

Don't forget to ask them *why* they think these people might be your Target Readers.

s. *Keywords* –

Do your Amazon and Kindle keywords give you hints about who might be your Target Markets?

t. *Book Theme* –

Does the theme of your book give you any ideas as to who would be interested in the topic?

One hint is to check the Encyclopedia of Associations and Gale's Catalogue for groups interested in the themes.

u. ***Book Characters* –**
What do your main characters do? This could lead you to groups who might be interested in your book.

v. ***Obstacles* –**
What obstacles do characters in your book face, and are there niche readers who would face similar obstacles? Perhaps they are potential Target Readers?

w. ***Affinity Groups* –**
What types of Affinity Groups would your groups of Target Market readers belong to?

24 There's Gold in Affinity Groups:

Affinity Groups that are geared to your book's theme or characters or plot line or general content, can become a ready source of active Target Readers and perhaps your Clan followers. Think of Affinity Groups that might have some connection to your book and its themes or characters.

25 What is an Affinity Group?

An Affinity Group is a small group of like-minded activists who work together on direct action to promote their own cause – check Wikipedia for more information on such groups.

There are thousands of Affinity Groups, clustered around shared backgrounds, professions, hobbies, passions, life stages, lifestyles, or shared political, moral or social beliefs.

26   Affinity Groups & Gladwell's Connectors:

Affinity Groups often have as members the type of individual that Malcolm Gladwell in his bestseller *The Tipping Point* calls **Connectors**.

Gladwell describes Connectors as people who know people, lots of them. And knows them well.

They have good links to a *wide and deep network*, are often the hubs of social networks, and can easily and quickly induce action in favor of causes common to the Connectors and their networks.

You are looking for Connectors to become your Target Readers and then to move on up to joining your Clan of followers.

So be constantly alert to spot them, wherever you meet them, and to make your pitch to them, followed by a request to sign up to your emails.

27   How to market to Affinity Groups:

The secret to marketing successfully to Affinity Groups is that people like to buy from people they like, and this willingness is much higher if the seller shares the same passions and interests as the buyer does, which is what happens with Affinity Group members.

Check this author's blog for his experiences with Affinity Groups:

http://plysandplus.wordpress.com/tag/affinity-marketing/

28   Search Often for Affinity Groups:

One of your Tasks in your Small Steps Plan must be to search for Affinity Groups related to your book, and to market to them.

29   Convert Target Readers into Clan:

Clan members are called different things by different people. Some writers call them their Tribe. Some call them a Community (with you as the central lynchpin).

Converting people from being a Target Reader to a follower and then into your Brand Ambassador is dealt with in detail in Task 4 below.

It all starts with *you asking your readers* to become members of your Clan; they do this by filling in the opt-in forms to subscribe for your regular emails and newsletters. Then you can ask them to consider becoming your "official" Brand Ambassadors, once you've explained what being an Ambassador does for them, and for you.

1   Introduction:

The aim of your Small Steps Plan is to identify your Target Readers, design means to reach them, persuade some of them to become members of your Clan of followers, and then to convert some of your Clan into your Brand Ambassadors.

Let's start by considering how one author, John Locke, achieved this through his promotion plan.

2   Who is John Locke?

Locke sold 1 million eBooks in 5 months, after taking time to study how the Kindle and Amazon markets work. A millionaire at 28, he bought an insurance company and later sold it; he then started writing books part time. At first he had little success selling eBooks, with 5 books written and very few sales in the first 8 months (highest sales were 27 copies in one month).

Then his new method kicked in, and everything changed.

His analysis of the eBook market made him conclude that if you chose your audience properly, knew what they wanted, and provided it to them, then the key battle was to get your targets to read _about_ your book, and if you did this, some (perhaps even 10%) might buy it.

3   Essence of the John Locke – Rabid Fans:

I recommend that you buy his book _How I sold 1 Million eBooks in five months,_ available on Amazon here:

http://www.amazon.com/John-Locke/e/B003ATT1YO

His book has several concrete plans about how to go about preparing your business plan – just a few of them are worth the price you will pay for his eBook.

Check out his Amazon Author site and make sure you read some of the many comments under the Reviews section of his books – some like him, some do not. Follow his blog and follow him on Twitter.

He came up with a method of marketing eBooks that helped him sell a million eBooks in his series; he calls it Loyalty Transfer.

This is Locke's view of fans: <u>you should aim at collecting *rabid* fans</u>.

His plan has four main elements:
- Have a Plan
- Know your Target Audience
- Take a Business Approach, and
- Use your tools (books, website, Twitter, blog) properly.

Locke writes that the basic tools you need are a book, a website, a Twitter account and a blog. You just have to learn how to use them properly.

4   Hints on Promotion from John Locke:

His advice on your focus as a self-published author is short and sweet: your job is to find your target readers, to write for them, and to turn them into what he calls **guaranteed buyers** of your coming books.

And the crux of his approach is summed up in two words – *Who* and *How*: he writes with his target audience in mind, and he knows how to find them. This comes through loudly and clearly in his book.

He spends the time to build up his **grass roots movement** of fans, and **builds his following one contact at a time**. Those fans then spread the word to their friends and so on.

5 John Locke on setting your Goals:

He sets project goals for himself, but <u>not</u> numbers of books sold.

<u>His first goal was to get five 5-star reviews, and a mailing list of 25 people who would buy his next book, and 100 *quality* Twitter followers.</u>

6 John Locke's Niche Marketing:

He is very, very clear on this: he writes for a specific audience and knows how to find them.

He recommends that authors profile their niche audiences just like an FBI profiler does when figuring out what kind of person committed the crime he is trying to solve.

<u>The narrower the niche, the better your chances of success</u>, he writes.

So he advises authors to find their *specific* audiences – because that specific audience is your niche; finding it is called target marketing.

John Locke says he has a dedicated audience of about 100,000 for his protagonist, Donovan Creed.

7 John Locke's Guaranteed Buyers:

He cultivates his relationships with his readers – and has 100 'quality' Twitter followers (he uses the word 'friends'), whom he has put on his *Guaranteed Buyer's List*. He started with 25, and now has over 1,000 Guaranteed Buyers, and writes that his ultimate target is a list of 10,000 Guaranteed Buyers.

Each time his books come out he sends short emails - less than a page - to 250 people a day and asks them to spread the word about the next book. The result is a burst of buying that propels his book up the Amazon lists and this generates more sales – a self-repeating process once you hit the Top 100, he says.

8   The John Locke Model:

The Locke model is:

Twitter TO Friends TO Buyers TO Reviewers.

9   John Locke's Friendship Circle:

Locke recommends using Twitter to create a Friendship Circle.

The idea is to convert the Twitter followers to become loyal friends and then to convert the loyal friends into buyers, and the buyers to reviewers.

The Friendship Circle gets him reviews and guaranteed buyers for future books. His Friendship Circle is his tribe.

What makes John Locke different from other authors who strive to form tribes of followers, is his disciplined attention to each and every one of his core fans – his Friendship Circle and 100 or so Twitter friends. He pays unrelenting attention to them, *through one on one discussions.*

10   John Locke and a Series of Books:

Read his reasons for deciding to write a series of books carefully – they make a lot of sense: you create synergy with your different ways of attracting your target audience. Also, readers like writers who have more than one book, because if they like the first one, there are more to read. And if they are there, these readers will go out and buy another. And another.

That's pretty strong support for writing a series of books.

11   **Your Clan of followers:**

Your Small Steps Plan starts with the assumption that you do not have John Locke's model up and working; nor do you have a traditional publishing company pushing you as author and your books; nor do you have built-in groupies who will snap up thousands of each book as you publish them.

So one of your first small steps is to build up your very own Clan of followers (your tribe), who will do for you what John Locke's Friendship Circle does for him.

You face severe challenges to rise above the hundreds of thousands of voices clamoring for attention on the Internet or Amazon or Kindle site. To become visible you need help.

And that's where the Clan of followers comes in.

They are an extension of your own Plan – unpaid, volunteer promoters, working for you.

It's using the leverage that all volunteer organizations use. Sweat equity by those who believe. John Locke calls it a *grass roots movement*. You want the enthusiasm of the few to ripple out to infect hundreds and thousands of others.

Your community will start off slowly, and grow slowly. Consider having your Team invite their relatives and friends to join it and participate in it, to kick start your Clan. Make sure you give them chances to look under the hood of your writing career, and your execution of your Plan. This <u>inside look</u> at your campaign could be a reward for many of your followers, especially if they can see that there is a two-way flow of interaction between you and them.

12   **What makes a Clan of Followers?**

<u>Engagement and nurturing</u>.

Go back and read once more about the John Locke model.

<u>The essence is **engagement**: giving them what they want as followers, involving them and using their ideas</u>.

One good way to do this is to try to put yourself in their shoes – do some role-playing and think like them.

Being able to engage authentically, consistently, and with the minimum of effort requires planning. Your Small Steps Plan helps you engage that way (with goals set, timing and content planned, and frequent tests of effectiveness included).

John Locke put it this way: love your readers and respond to them. For example, he answers <u>every</u> email.

What engages them?

Boring tweets turn people off. Constant self-promotion turns people off.

People need a reason to return to your blog posts or tweets or Facebook Page. They need to feel they <u>benefit</u> from – and are <u>recognized</u> for - doing this.

You need to personalize your social network presence, and be courteous, just as you would if you were face to face with that person. If they complimented you by referring your blog post to someone else, or retweeted or mentioned your, would you not thank them for doing it? Or return the compliment by reciprocating?

Rewarding your readers who respond to your is another way to say thank you; we deal with rewards below.

A big part of successful tribe building is the ability to meet the needs of those who participate in social networks.

13   Playing in Social Network Sandboxes:

If you want to participate successfully in social networks, you need to meet what I believe are the 3 main needs of other people who are playing in these social network sandboxes:

- ***entertainment*** - they want to be entertained (why is YouTube so popular?);
- ***nurturing their friends*** - they want to find things to send to their own friends so that they are entertained (that's why there are so many retweets); or
- ***learning*** - they want to learn something (either for their own sake, or to stay current in their social interactions).

14   How to build your Clan:

You build your tribe in two main ways: Engagement and Rewards.

15   Building your tribe by Engaging them:

This is a summary of some methods to engage your readers; each part of the Small Steps Plan discussed in the other parts of this book has its own collection of methods to engage readers.

You build your tribe one contact at a time (see John Locke's experience), so don't expect huge results in a short time.

And it takes one contact at a time because you are trying to establish a one-on-one relationship with readers you don't know, will never meet, and who have many other opportunities to be amused or intrigued.

You have to become visible to your readers. Once you are visible, you have to be there so they can see you.

16   Use Cyberspace Conversation Spaces:

Engagement simply means getting into the conversations in such a way that others want to talk to you. Social networks like Twitter and the Forums create their own conversation spaces – cyberspace public gathering spots where like-minded people can huddle together and talk about things.

You want those in the cyberspace conversation spaces to recognize your entry into the conversation (your Author Brand is designed to make you stand out from the crowd), to listen to you, and to respond to you. What you say, when you say it, how you say it, and why you say it are all important elements of what you bring to the conversation space: if others like your elements, they will stop and listen.

If they don't, they will ignore you and move on.

17   Building your tribe by Rewarding them:

People love rewards, if they are given for the right reasons, are the right kind of rewards, and hold no downsides for the receiver.

Giving rewards this way to your readers is one of the most important arts you need to learn to succeed in meeting your Promotion Plan goals.

Give people your free eBooks, many say. That'll generate name recognition for you, and this should lead to sales of your books. Not so. Your gifting program needs to have follow through: simply casting your bread upon the waters only leads to your bread drifting for a while and then sinking to the bottom. You need to know what you are trying to achieve before you start any gift or reward program.

This means thinking it through, setting goals in your promotion Plan, and monitoring your efforts to make sure you are achieving your goals.

You might give free eBooks in order to attract attention to the other books in your series of books.

18   Examples of Possible Rewards:

a. *Courtesy* –
One major reward to all those joining the cyberspace conversations is for participants to obey the etiquette. Make sure you do this.

b. *Thanks* –
Another major reward for someone who has done something that benefits you or the Indie Community, is to recognize them and say thanks. You can do this by saying thanks, by mentioning them, or by Retweeting them in turn, or through a Direct Message to them on Twitter).

c. *Involvement* –

Adopt as one of your principles of your Author Brand your commitment to improve the Indie Community. Think how you might help the person you wish to reward by involving them or recognizing them in the Indie Community, and making them part of an enlargement and enhancement of that community.

For example, it they have their own blog, could you kill two birds with one stone by inviting them to do some joint blogging with you. Or by reviewing their book on your new book review blog or on Amazon. Or by tagging their books or mentioning them on Twitter.

d. *Indie Recognition Award* –

Or perhaps you could team up with other author bloggers to establish an Indie Community recognition award? You and your co-founders decide on recipients – after asking your own readers for suggestions – and publicly recognize those who have in the past quarter done something worthwhile that benefits all independently published authors. Ask eBook authors to agree to donate one of their free eBooks to the winners (and publicize the list of such donors and their books).

What you are looking for are innovative ways to recognize and reward your readers, rather than just doing what others are doing.

e. *Gifting e-information* –

Google *Amazon books and rewards* and *Amazon book advisers*, for hints.

Several suggest putting together a package of e-information gifts for those who buy your book within a certain timeframe, or do something else. The essence of such prizes is that the prizes are to be worthwhile to people, but cost free to the donors (who write or gather the free e-information articles used as prizes).

If you go this route, make sure the e-information is valuable. Check it out with your Dream Teams.

It might be worthwhile to cooperate with other Indie authors to jointly prepare some really good e-information packages that you can all use as rewards.

Think about e-information on how to publish books, self-publishing, setting up books clubs that really work, tweets that work, lists of things they might be interested in, and other topics that your Target Reader Personas might like.

Many such gifts rely on the principle known as the *psychology of second interest* (PSI) – some will buy your book or provide an email address and consent to future emails or agree to retweet your selected tweets or mention your blog post in their blog etc., in order to get the free bonus product.

It's a means to sweeten the deal; think air miles. It can be used as an inducement to do something, or as a retention tool to keep a customer.

It's also known as 'free cookies' marketing – see this article for more on it:

http://www.psychotactics.com/is-your-marketing-missing-the-cookie-factor

The writer defines free cookies this way in that article:

"This in short is the *cookie factor*. You create a demand for the product with something so alluring that the customer forgets the product itself and concentrates mainly on the *cookies*. Psychologists call this the *psychology of second interest*. This effectively means that people shift focus onto the goodies and end up buying the main product based on this tiny inducement."

f. *Follow them* –

On Twitter, and send them a direct message <u>explaining exactly why</u> you are following them.

g. *Follow Friday* –

Show new followers you appreciate their following you by asking others on Follow Friday to follow them using #ff – just make sure you give a good reason why people should follow someone or it's just garbage.

h. *Ask* –

Ask your readers what kinds of rewards they think people might like, and for links to sites or blog posts with lists of rewards.

i. *Extracts* –

If you want to reward or recognize an author who benefited you or the Indie Community, consider posting an article on your own blog with an extract from that author's work that stirred you, along with links to the author's author blog. I call this the *Quote Gift*.

j. *Author At Work Peeks* –

I call these *Soul Gifts*, because they allow your selected readers to peek into your soul as a writer.

Many writers just do not realize how much non-writers hold them in high regard. We come from a literary society, where the written word and writers are valued. Many people are fascinated by the art of creation that goes into any novel, by the problems faced by writers, by curiosity about just where they got their ideas.

So compile a gift package consisting of your **Author At Work Peeks**, only given to the special few. These would be those who benefit you, or have agreed to become your Author Ambassadors, or given you their email addresses and agreed to receive messages from you, or have agreed to gift a copy of your eBook to at least one relative or friend or random choice recipient.

In your very own **Author At Work Peeks** you could describe how you came to write, what you write about, how you plan your books, where you seek inspiration, where ideas come from, how you go about writing, what help you get (don't forget to acknowledge and to introduce – with their prior consent – members of your Team, along with photos of them), how many drafts you do, how you revise your work, what other writers you follow on Twitter or their author blogs, what forums you participate in, how you prepare for your participation, how your Promotion Plan is working out, your writing journal entries etc.

Include deleted scenes with explanations of why you took them out (and of the struggle to do that – it broke my heart to wrestle our first drafts of **Obelisk Seven** down from around 250,000 words to less than 100,000).

Some writers now write up *interviews with their characters*, which give readers with access to them an understanding of what the characters are thinking, their backgrounds, hopes, plans, and fears.

If, like me, you use *photos of places and things* to give you ideas when you are writing, why not share some of them with your readers?

In other words, the rubber hits the road, nitty gritty of writing.

And invite other writers to provide you with snippets about their writing habits and journey, as well – this boosts the Indie Community.

k. **Prequels** –

Your special readers get advance examples of chapters from your forthcoming books.

l. **Input** –

Think about inviting your special readers (your tribe or clan members) to be a party to the act of creation of your future books and/or blog posts.

Make it clear any ideas they give you are yours to use, free of charge, and they have no share in the book or its copyright. Invite suggestions for characters or places, perhaps even subplots. Test various alternatives with them. Poll them for input about what they think works best, and why. Consider mentioning them in the dedication page. How else can you engage your readers by inviting them to join the creative process?

m. **Guinea Pigs** –

Perhaps you might need some readers to serve as guinea pigs that allow you to test various items of future works with them? If they become one of your Guinea Pigs, you can get their views on scenes, characters, plots, promotional ideas, your Author Brand, your Target Reader Persona definitions, your author and book video drafts etc.

How many kinds of involvement can you think of for your Guinea Pigs?

Take some time to talk over the selection criteria of your Guinea Pigs with your Team. Can just anyone become one? Or do readers earn their way in through various steps (retweets of your tweets, other promotion steps they took, comments on your blogs and forum posts etc.) Make sure you have a handful lined up before you launch your Guinea Pigs plan, to avoid embarrassment.

n.   *Market testing* –

You might reserve this for your Guinea Pigs, or go wider and let every reader participate. You could test the suitability of your ideas for a book for the Dream Team Personas you developed. Is there a fit? If not, what needs to be changed? You would need to provide a summary of the future book, and of your Personas to make this one work.

o.   *Kill the Jargon* –

Ask your Brand Ambassadors to help you strip any jargon out of your promotional messages to make them clearer, simpler, with more emotional and power words and so more effective. Reward those who reply.

What about testing what works and does not work in your existing book(s)?

p.   *Newsletter(s)* –

Perhaps you could do with two kinds: one for everyone who provides you with an email address and consent to receive future emails and messages, and another for your more select group (those who have 'officially' joined your Clan of followers by requesting a certificate from you confirming that they are members, which they can print and keep; or your Guinea Pigs; or some other selection criteria – such as early responders to your surveys or Early Wave Buyers of your eBook).

Your e-zine would cover items of interest to you and to your readers.

You could invite guest contributors of articles for your Newsletters, and/or boost the Indie Community by agreeing on an article swap deal for a certain period with other writers who have Newsletters of their own. Check author newsletters to get ideas of what to put in yours.

q. *Checklists* –

I am a great believer in checklists for tasks or problem solving, and use them whenever I can.

Think of your Target Reader Personas – what problems or issues might they have that could be eased if they only had a good checklist or two or three to guide them? Could you come up with some and use them to reward your Followers?

r. *Summary* –

If your book is a technical one (like this one), consider offering a short summary of your book as a reward.

s. *Interviews* –

Check this site for how to use interviews (video or recorded telephone interviews with people related to your book) as rewards:

http://www.magnet4web.com/content/marketing-2/5-exceptional-bonuses-that-will-increase-your-sales-.php

Spend time brainstorming with your Team about how to make your rewards unique, interesting, costless and effective. Give them the WOW factor.

More on Brand Ambassadors:

19   Conversion into Brand Ambassadors:

Your stock in trade is your brand as an author and your books. Your aim is to *leverage your reach* by converting dozens and later on hundreds of readers who have read your books into your Clan members and then some of them into your Brand Ambassadors.

You want your Brand Ambassadors to go out of their way to help promote your books by telling everyone about you and them, using their own social networks and word of mouth to do so. That is exactly what John Locke's fans do for him.

20   Why use Brand Ambassadors?

TIP: Google *12 reasons you need brand ambassadors now social horsepower* for an article with good hints why you need to use Ambassadors.

TIP: Google *top 100 influencers in social media social-technologyreview* for some information on influencers.

21   How to Name your Ambassadors:

You could call them Brand Ambassadors, but that begs the question: What brand? For them to self-identify with the name, they need one *they* find attractive. Ask yourself about any name you choose: Would I feel comfortable telling my friends I was [your name for the group]?

Find a name that is positive, but neutral (that is, not necessarily directly linked to your name, as this might discourage some of your Clan from signing up as an Ambassador). John Locke's choice of Friendship Circle is a good one: I can see people saying proudly that they are a member of John Locke's Friendship Circle, after he was established as an eBook writer.

Employees are *motivated by working for a common purpose*; being part of a larger process also gives them satisfaction. This is true of Ambassadors as well. John Locke's tweets show that he is pushing his identification *as an Indie self-publisher*, and asking for potential readers to join his Friendship Circle if they want to support him, *because* he is a self-publisher.

Consider whether you should use a name which indicates to the world that the Ambassador is a supporter of the Indie Community, as a matter of principle. It's the old David and Goliath tussle: give them a chance to become Davids; and stick it to the Goliath-man. Us versus Them, and In Unity there is Strength.

How about the title *Indie Goodwill Ambassador*? Or just *Indie Ambassador*? Or *Indie Ninjas*? How about SMBA (*Social Media Brand Ambassador*)?

22 What drives a person to become a Brand Ambassador?

Here's Ted Rubin's advice on Ambassadors:

"It's up to you to provide something more compelling than a pretty Facebook page or Twitter profile. When customers seek you out via social, they're looking for an opportunity to build an emotional connection. So give it to them... Your existing or future customers won't become brand advocates by simply being your customers. They need to have an experience that stands out. So don't be routine in your interactions. Be remarkable! Make it a part of your culture and brand DNA. That happens on an individual basis, and it's different for everyone. You can't mass-produce it."

Google *How to Turn Relationships Into Brand Advocacy Ted Rubin* for the post.

23   Stuff the Diplomatic Pouches of your Brand Ambassadors with Goodies:

Once you have a few Brand Ambassadors, make sure you give them plenty of goodies to use in their spreading the word about you and your Indie journey and your books.

Use your email messages to them to provide them with material for their **Diplomatic Pouches**:

- easily shareable and emailable PDFs with stories of your journey;
- helpful hints for readers and others; and
- things that add to the reputation of your Brand Ambassadors.

When deciding on Rewards, did you meet one or more of the 3 main needs of people who use social networks (entertainment; nurturing their friends; or learning)?

24   The Loyalty Ripple Effect:

Ambassadors provide you as a writer with the benefits of the *Loyalty Ripple Effect*. Your efforts to promote your brand and your books is like a single pebble tossed into a big pond; you will create ripples. Now think of several people joining in tossing their pebbles into your pond, and even better, into their own ponds, and the ripples moving outwards in every pond.

This means you and your Team need to find Ambassadors who can toss pebbles about your book into big ponds they can access. You need to go pond-hunting. Every Ambassador who throws a pebble into her pond by spreading word about your book, is an appreciating asset for you.

Any Clan member who co-creates one of your messages is more likely to become a co-promoter, with pebbles into their own ponds.

The Ripple Effect is not new; traditionally lawyers, doctors and architects have relied heavily on this as their best promotion avenue for their services.

25 **Bigger Ripples with Empowered Involvement:**

If you give your Ambassadors an active say and a role in the selling of your books, this will increase the Ripple Effect. John Locke takes advantage of this with his promotion methods.

TIP: Google *the ripple effect 3 keys to success for selling in social media paul marsden* for an interesting discussion of this.

26 **Ripples work better if they Care:**

Research has shown that those who care about the product being sold *because* it is personally important and relevant to them, will advocate for the products.

This is another reason why you should consider becoming an Indie Community supporter, and linking that to your calls to action; see above for the discussion of John Locke and his help-the-indie-market tweets.

Simply asking people in a polite way to help spread the word has been found to be very effective in generating ripples.

Google *caring is sharing how to get your brand advocates to care* for some good hints on how this can increase the ripple effect.

Some brand advocates share for four reasons:
- they love the brand;
- the brand makes *them* look good or smart;
- they want to help others; and
- they like the content.

How can you use these 4 drivers to fashion your calls to action to potential brand advocates? Talk about it with your Teams and your Clan.

Once again, if promoting the Indie Community (while also promoting you as a member of that Community) makes people look smart or good, why not add this aspect to some of your messages?

27   Where and how to find Ambassadors:

The wider her platform is, the better for you, because she will reach them with positive news about you, or copies of your blog posts etc. So pay some attention to their outreach when weighing their quality as an ambassador for you.

If you are deciding how much time to devote to cultivating a possible Ambassador, you should track the social network activities of your potential and actual Ambassadors, to see the degree of their engagement, which will link back to the reach of your own promotion campaign.

How do you do this?

Try the free application of *Topsy.com*. Topsy, now belonging to Apple, has an index of Twitter tweets going back to its start in 2006, and so can give you some information on past tweets of the prospective Ambassador.

For current reach, become a follower of the Ambassador and see what she is doing.

TIP: Google *69 Free Social Media Monitoring Tools priit kallas* for some free measurement tools to discuss with your Team and ask your Clan for their views on. Check out *followerwonk* which is a free social media tool to search for influential bloggers.

Google *9 Reasons Your Company Should Use Brand Advocates: New Research* for a good article by socialmediaexaminer on how to do enroll your email subscribers as your *Brand Ambassadors*.

Note that asking your readers to become your brand advocates or Brand Ambassadors might satisfy one of the 3 major needs from social networks (entertainment; nurturing their friends; or learning).

One study found that 54% of brand advocates viewed the sharing of information as a type of relaxation, and were 83% more likely to share information with others.

28 How to get and keep Ambassadors:

TIP: Ask your Team if they have any relatives or friends that might want to learn how to become brand advocates, and enroll them as guinea pigs in your pilot project to launch your **Indie Ambassador 101** series of lessons. Then roll out the Lessons to your broad Clan.

As one writer put it, the key to keeping your Influencers happy is remembering that you're in a relationship, and relationships are all about give and take.

You have to give, not just take.

So brainstorm ideas, try to be different, aim for engagement, freshness, and compulsion.

29   **Here are some ways to give:**

   a.   Your giving should be of value to your potential Ambassador. For starters, the unwritten rule of reciprocity demands that you promote your Ambassadors as they promote you.

   b.   Google *ways to turn customers into brand ambassadors* for some articles you can scan to find 3 to 5 ideas you can discuss with your Team and your own Ambassadors

   c.   When pitching to Clan members to become your Ambassadors, you might need a Brand Ambassador elevator pitch. Google *6 Essentials for Making Your Elevator Pitch Unforgettable Larry Alton* for some hints on such an elevator speech.

   d.   TIP: Google *How to Turn Loyal Customers into Brand Ambassadors Gini Dietrich* for some very good ideas about how to launch your conversion of Clan members into Brand Ambassadors.

   e.   Gini Dietrich includes these solid hints:

- Updates on a page for them to use in their ponds;
- A short video of you that they can use in their promotion, that spells out what you are trying to achieve;
- Offer to guest blog with the Ripplers.

f. TIP: *You, Your Clan & GroupTweet* - Consider using GroupTweet for tweets to one Twitter account from your Clan members, and/or your Brand Ambassadors, and/or your virtual Book Club, and/or your Writers Club. Make this a task in your Small Steps Plan.

g. GroupTweet lets from 2 to 100,000 people send tweets to one Twitter account. You can moderate the messages and arrange the scheduling for the tweets. You can have the tweeters identified or their names hidden. Brainstorm with your Dream Team of advisors and Brand Ambassadors how best to use GroupTweet in your Twitter Plan. You could select themes and have the Clan grouptweet about it. Use GroupTweet to hold your Twitter Debates with only Clan members being able to tweet?

h. Or they can *Join-a-Tribe* by agreeing to become a signed up member of your Clan of Clan followers. Perhaps they *Wanna be an Ambassador?* and will join as one of your Brand Ambassadors. Or they might want to *Guide the Tribe* by sending you some tips or advice on how to engage your Target Readers.

i. If you ask them to *Flesh Them Out*, they might comment on the features of your Target Readers Personas.

j. Consider a series of book videos, dealing with your Indie Journey (introducing yourself as author, your book, your book's characters, your own Writers Club, your overall Promotion Plan, your Team, some of your Brand Ambassadors, your Target Readers reading from your book etc.).

k. How about helping your Ambassadors make Video testimonials of you and/or your books?

l. Offer to join *their* Brand Ambassador group – perhaps on a reciprocal basis?

m. Offer to beta-read a chapter of their future book(s).

30   Use UGC to generate buzz:

Showcase any UGC (user generated content) you get from your readers, in a blog post or FB or hashtag gallery, and link to it often. Google *UGC 101: Guide to User-Generated Content Marketing wordstream* for hints on how to go about this.

What is UGC? It is endless, and includes: blog comments; user generated blog posts; reviews of your book; reviews of your Small Steps Plan promotion campaigns; user generated videos; forum posts; podcasts; Facebook comments and posts.

Google *where to find user generated content* to see if you can use some for your own purposes.

If you organize any contests, perhaps require some UGC related to your books or your messages as a condition for entry, plus giving yourself the right to use it for your own purposes.

Google *Know Your Audience – The Secret To Author John Locke's Success Caitlin muir* also Google *John Locke the asterisked legacy of a million-seller author* for a list of Locke's main steps.

Your Small Steps Plan includes two major channels that contain information about you and your activities: your Amazon Author Page, and your Author Blog.

TIP: I suggest you carry with you at all times a little notebook – *My Bloggy Book* – and jot down any ideas you get for blog posts, keywords, keyword phrases, and headings.

1   What is your Amazon Author Page?

You start Amazon Author Page by going here:
https://authorcentral.amazon.com/gp/home
Through the Author Central site you can click on your books on Amazon and claim them by providing your email.

You get a very handy site address for your author page, which you can use in all your blogs etc. – here's mine:
https://www.amazon.com/author/glennashton
Note that your name as an author is identified with the Amazon.com site – that's nifty for you. Print that hyperlink on all your letterheads, and on your business cards that introduce you as an author.

This is the site that readers can go to, to buy your Amazon and Kindle books. Make sure it is easily available in all your social network channels.

You decide what to put in your Author Page, so you can ensure that its content reflects your Author Brand. The Author Page is free and helps you get your name out there. The Author Page helps with Amazon searches by readers who input your name. They will find your Page and can dip into your marketing information. You also can track your sales rankings through Author Central.

You sign in using your Amazon account.

Your biography is needed as well as your photo. You can also link your Page to your Author Blog – by adding an RSS feed on the Author Page. All your Author Blog posts will appear on your Amazon Author Page soon after you posted them.

You can link your Page to your Twitter feed, and upload one of your Author Videos – the video itself, not the link to it.

Your Book Description is also entered.

2   What is an Author Blog?

You blog is your means to spread the message to the market place about you, as author, and your books.

A blog (also known as Web logs, shortened to blog) is an online journal that is updated by an entry called a post. Someone who writes a blog is called a blogger.

3   Do you need both a Blog and a Website?

I don't think you need both. Websites are more complex than blogs, both to start and to maintain. I recommend that your start with a blog and later on decide if you need a website.

My blog is free, and is built using Blogger which is now owned by Google.

Wordpress is another good blogger site.

Blogger provides free templates you can use to kick start your own Author Blog.

4   Goals of your own Author Blog:

You should have *three primary goals* in this part of your Plan (readers signing up to get your emails, joining your Clan, and converting into your Brand Ambassadors).

5   More Goals of the Author:

These additional goals should cover aspects dealt with in this Task, including:

- the number of posts you will write;
- the timing of your posts;
- topics to be covered (matched against your Target Readers Personas);
- proper treatment of any comments you receive;
- starting to link to your own posts and to external links;
- size variations of your posts (number of words);
- use of proper images;
- guest blogging;
- post swapping with members of the Indie Community you are cooperating with;
- participating in blog tours as well as starting your own blog tour;
- doing some research into your competitors' blogs;
- planning steps to engage your Target Readers; and
- periodic reviews of the effectiveness of your blog posts with your Dream Team advisors.

6   The Author Blog as Landing Pad:

I recommend that you use your Author Blog as the Landing Pad or Hub of your whole social media outreach. It's a place readers and others can go to find out about you and your books.

If you want to see some ideas I used on my Author Blog to have it perform as a Landing Pad for readers, check it out (http://glennashton.blogspot.com).

You should Google other authors, especially your competition, and jot down what you like about their blogs. As time goes on you can experiment with changes to your first few designs.

7   Target Markets for your Author Blog:

Your Author Blog must be designed to appeal to your target audience: you want them to buy your book, visit your blog again, follow you on Twitter, read your Facebook page, and come back to buy more books you write.

To do this, you need to establish an emotional link with your blog readers: they need to know what's in your book that they might like (the benefit), to read about your personal experience on your journey as a writer, and your hopes.

Read Task 3 and 4 about making sure your messages appeal to your Target Reader Personas.

8   Help your Target Readers post your Blog to Social Networks:

You can do this easily by adding social media buttons to each of your Author Blog posts. Your readers can then click on the buttons to boost your blog post by having it sent to the social media.

You should add at the bottom of each post in capital letters this action call: *Please help me boost my author blog by clicking on one or more of these buttons.*

I use the large buttons in the article by Harish entitled *Add Beautiful Social Bookmarking Widget (CSS/jQuery) for Blogger / Blogspot.*

The big buttons appear on the bottom of each of your posts. The buttons are for Facebook, Twitter, GoogleBuzz, StumbleUpon, Digg, Delicious, LinkedIn, Reddit and Technorati. Later on, you should join each of these social networks.

Google *Add Beautiful Social Bookmarking Widget (CSS/jQuery) for Blogger / Blogspot Harish* for the detailed instructions.

9   How to Start your Author Blog:
How often should you post –

You need to settle on a publication schedule for your posts – once you've posted a few entries. Experiment with the timing – every 3 days? Once a week? Several times a week? And then decide.

Your Book –

Consider material in your book: can you use part of it in your introductory posts? Make sure your initial posts give readers information about your book: genre, published on both Amazon and Kindle, word count, your Elevator and Author Speeches, themes, characters.

Purposes –

And spell out your purposes with your Author Blog – don't be too shy to explain your three primary goals:

getting email addresses to you can (with their consent) keep them in the know about you and your book; having them join your Clan of Followers; and converting some of them to become your Brand Ambassadors.

Steps –

Read this series of 6 articles from *dummies.com* entitled *The Essentials of Using Blogger to Publish your Blog*, about the actual steps you need to take to create your first blog using Blogger:

http://www.dummies.com/how-to/content/how-to-create-your-first-blog-using-blogger.html
http://www.dummies.com/how-to/content/the-essentials-of-using-blogger-to-publish-your-bo.html

Dip into this site for some hints on starting up your blog:

http://www.unrulyguides.com/2012/04/blogging-basics-for-writers/

The articles in *unrulyguides.com* are worth exploring. Note his recommendation that you take Small Steps when starting your blog, and his advice on your blogging goals – can you use some of his goals in your Plan?

10   How to build a successful Author Blog: Personalizing your Blog:

Blogger templates give you a choice of layouts and design, which you can adopt as is, or start changing to suit your own taste.

You might get some ideas on how to format your blog from this *dummies.com* article headed How to Format a Blog:

http://www.dummies.com/how-to/content/how-to-format-a-blog.html

Here's one good tip from it:

"If your blog looks a bit boring, then you need to format it. Knowing how to format a blog can improve visual impact and readability: You can break up long blocks of text, add styling headers and line breaks, and use paragraphs to improve the flow of posts. You can also emphasize text by using italics and bold."

This *dummies.com* article gives some ideas for how to personalize your own blog even if you are using one of the Blogger templates:

http://www.dummies.com/how-to/content/how-to-design-and-customize-your-blog.html

You can change the four distinct areas of your blog (logo, headers, sidebars, footers).

Choose one of the Blogger templates to start, and change it once you have the hang of posting to your blog. Discuss the layout and design (colors, images, title of the blog etc.) with your Team.

11   Think about your Author Blog Title:

Does it fit with your Author Brand? Is it distinctive enough? Does it identify you at a glance? Is it easy to remember?

12   How to Pull Readers to your Author Blog: Make your Blog Post titles say WOW

The title or headline of any post to your blog is a crucial element in attracting readers. If it hooks the reader, they will linger and read your post; if it does not hook them, they will move on with a click of their mouse.

You have between 3 and 5 seconds to hook your readers with your blog post title.

Experiment with two or three headlines for a blog post or tweet to see which work best.

Copy Huffington Post's ways by asking your readers to give you a better headline for a blog post or tweet referring to a blog post of yours. Asking your Brand Ambassadors for headlines for future blog posts is another means to engage them.

This article from *dummies.com* has some hints for attention grabbing headlines for websites:

http://www.dummies.com/how-to/content/how-to-use-effective-title-tags-for-better-ranking.html

Here is one hint from it: write unique titles and make sure they are keyword-rich.

And keep your title short because Google cuts off the title after 70 characters so you need to get your message into your first seventy.

Sharpen your headline hook by making it a List (8 Ways to do X)

Start your very own collection of *Headlines that Hook* and add to it examples from other blogs, tweets, newspapers, magazines and book chapter headings, and articles on choosing headlines.

13   Headlines that Hook

What and how your headline reads is very, very, very critical: if your headline is blah, they will move on to something else.

Use teasers to pull traffic in twitter and blog post headings.

Read this article by Bob Dunn titled *10 Ways to Get More Blog Traffic with Social Media Teasers,* for hints on how to hook readers with your blog headlines:

http://www.blogworld.com/2012/11/28/10-ways-to-get-more-blog-traffic-with-social-media-teasers/

Take time to write and re-write the heading. The content of the body comes later, but the heading is what hooks them.

Tell them what to expect from your post – Dunn's example of a headline that does this is *Get two dozen unique blog post ideas in 15 minutes with this simple technique.* Now that is pretty good, not so?

Dunn's other suggestions (with illustrations) are:

- Use a healthy dose of fear;
- Ask a question;
- Don't give away all your secrets;
- Take an opposite view;
- Promise an insider's secret;
- Make 'em laugh;
- Pull the curtain back; and
- Make a unique comparison.

Check blogs by others, and note which ones hooked you, and what they had that made them work.

Google *good headlines for blog posts* for more hints from others. Note how so many of them hold a promise of something that helps make them irresistible.

Check this site for more hints on headlines that hook (note especially the one of the series that talks about promising benefits; the one about ten headline formulas that work, and the one about why starting your headline with *Why* is a good idea):

http://www.copyblogger.com/magnetic-headlines/

Try this headliner hooker for your tweets or blog posts – How to Do This and Get that Benefit e.g.: *How to Win Friends and Influence* People, by Napoleon Hill.

Ask your Target Readers to send you (via email or by comments on your blog posts or by direct messages on Twitter) good examples for your new *Headlines that Hook* collection.

Run a competition in your blog or on your Facebook Page or via Twitter for best *Headlines that Hook* (use the hashtag #headlinesthathook). Offer a free eBook or other reward (see 6.4 for reward ideas).

14   Use comments to interact with Readers:

The number and quality of the comments on your blog posts is a surefire indication whether you are engaging your readers.

Many blog comments = Engagement

You should respond to blog comments you get on your Author Blog. Do not sit out while others take part in the conversation in your comments section of your blog.

What you are aiming at is to turn the *dialogue* between you and the first commentator, into a *macrologue* by having other readers pile into the discussion by adding their two bits' worth. And you do this by showing appreciation to everyone who joins in, and then helping the conversation to flow.

How do you make the macrologue flow?

You do it the same way you would do if it was a real life conversation between you and others.

You acknowledge the contribution of others.

If there's a lull, you point out some ideas given by earlier commentators and steer the conversation that way to see if there's more traction to be gained going there.

One way to do this can take the form of *contrasting* in a few words any comments by others that oppose each other. *John said X, but Mary said Y. Anyone have any thoughts on how to bridge this?*

Or you use *agreement – I'm with Mary on this point, and add this to her [your idea].... What do you think, John?*

TIP: Google *how to make conversations flow*, and write down some of the hints you like in your *My Bloggy Book* for later use.

Thank people for taking part, and invite them to join in again in future.

One way to get that critical first comment?

- Ask a question at the end of your post.
- Give alternative views and ask for readers to choose and say why.

TIP: Don't forget to help your fellow Indie Community members get the flow going in their blog posts by commenting there; this could result in reciprocity on your blog.

If there are several macrologues taking place in the blogosphere on the same or similar topics, don't forget to refer to those you like in your comments in your own blog. *Over at A's Blog Jonty argues that X = Y; check it out.*

Make a point of scanning blogs your like to see if they are talking about the same topics you are blogging about, and refer to those conversations.

15   Follow your commentators:

Do your homework on the best commentators on your blog.

Your aim is _ongoing conversations (engagement)_ with your Target Readers, so that you can convert them into your Clan Followers and then into your Brand Ambassadors.

So if someone takes the time to comment on your blog post click on their name and read their profile; go to their blog and join in their macrologues, if it suits your Author Brand. Up tweet their macrologues, and recommend them to your Twitter followers.

16   Recognizing your Commentators:

If you end up with lively comments on your blog, thank them by occasionally featuring some of them and the commentators in a blog post.

Thank people for commenting, and talk about the conversations that took place about your topics, who stood out, etc. This acknowledges their contribution and recycles the macrologue in a different way.

TIP: Blog about _Headlines that Hook_ using examples from your own collection. Don't forget to acknowledge by name your Target Readers who gave you any examples you use.

Comments are the gold mine of blogging. Here's what the dummies.com article says about comments:

"Blogging isn't only about writing; _it's about inducing other people to respond, either on one's own blog or in another blog_. The macrologue, the big blogging conversation, encourages bloggers not only to participate but to hope for an influential role in that conversation and compete for it."

Read the article at:

http://www.dummies.com/how-to/content/using-comments-in-blogs.html

Join the macrologue, the big blogging conversation in the sky. Express your views; invite the views of others.

17   Learn from comments on your competitors' blogs:

Study the comments on your competitors' blogs to get an idea about what readers want to talk about: can you join the macrologue by posting on the same topics, but with your own unique twist to it?

See this article for some hints on what to look for on the blogs of others:

http://www.dummies.com/how-to/content/how-to-learn-from-lurking-on-other-blogs.html

Note down what you like and what seems to work well on those blogs in your _My Bloggy Book_.

18   Learn from the Experts:

Check what works, as in this article by students from the Stanfield Graduate School of Business:

http://en.blog.wordpress.com/2012/04/17/how-to-get-more-page-views-for-your-blog/

Among their findings for pulling more readers to blogs? Making your blog easy to follow; frequent and regular posts.

When it comes to blogs, fresh is good, so update your Author Blog often. You want your Target Readers to make checking your Author Blog a regular (preferably daily) habit.

19 Size of your Posts:

Many are smallish (250 to 500 words) but you can make them much longer if what you want to say is interesting enough to hold the attention of your readers, and needs more room.

Make long posts visually attractive by using bold subheadings in the body of your post.

20 Track your Progress:

See what works and what does not work on your own blog, by monitoring it carefully. What is measured, improves. So measure yourself.

Keywords help convert bounces (landings on the blog post), into conversions (readers who linger and read the post and perhaps comment on it). Experiment with them.

Blogger Stats allows you to check page views per post for different periods, and ranks posts per page views per period, and allows you to see where the traffic came from, and the geographic location of your blog readers. What can you and your Team learn from these? If some topics reach a lot more readers than others, revisit the topics in future blog posts. If it works, do it again, and again …

If you are cooperating with other Indie Community members on mutual promotion (or are a member of

Triberr) see what keywords and keyword phrases, head-lines and topics, work best for them.

Dip into this article from dummies.com about using a spreadsheet program to generate high traffic keywords for your site – how can you use it for your blog?

http://www.dummies.com/how-to/content/use-a-spreadsheet-program-to-generate-high-traffic.html

Boost your publishers, Amazon and Kindle, by writing blog posts about them (include their names in your head-ings).

21   YOU are the Reason:

You're the reason - Make your Target Readers return to you by making yourself interesting in your Author Blog.

Blog posts that attract *return visitors* are those that make your Target Readers more interested in you, your brand, or what you have to say about your niche.

It's worth repeating: They need to be interested in YOU!

Tell them about your take on things, your journey as a writer, your obstacles, sessions with your Team and what you did after that and how it worked out, your wrestling with your definitions of your Target Readers Personas – and ask for help and hints and ideas.

Captivate them, make them want to go with you on your journey, become part of the team, to join up as a Brand Ambassador.

Ask your Team how you can make yourself ultra-interesting to your Target Readers.

For some ideas on how to personalize yourself to your Target Readers go to the blog of Drew Berman, and check the heading *21 Blog Post Ideas that Ooze YOU!*:

http://blog.drewberman.com/millionaire-mind/blog-post-ideas/

I particularly liked his idea for blog posts on what and how *you* are doing *in your niche*, what is and is not working, lessons that could be learned, celebrating your wins.

Note his request to retweet his post – please do so if you liked it.

22   Go for the Excitement in your blog posts:

This article from *dummies.com* has some hints for how to add excitement to your blog posts:

http://www.dummies.com/how-to/content/write-exciting-and-engaging-web-content-for-better.html

You need to *show, not tell*, the article explains:

"Your Web site needs to persuade people, interest them, and draw them in with good content. For this reason, *you should write as if they're there*, not just reading about an event after the fact."

It advises using *sensory words* (make your readers *feel* it not just read it), and being *specific*, giving details, for more impact.

23   Content is King:

Readers want information of the kind *they* want, so you have to put yourself in the shoes of your Target Readers Personas when writing posts. Jot down the types of questions you think these Personas would ask you about your topics, and then answer them.

Include some **evergreen topics** in your ***Editorial Content Plan***.

One recommendation I found that I liked was to prepare a short list of evergreen topics (topics which are not time-sensitive) and write posts on them which you can use at later dates. You could focus on your Author Brand and/or your Target Readers Personas, and draw up a list of topics which would appeal to them.

TIP: Include in your *Editorial Content Plan* a calendar with some dates for you to write a handful of these evergreen topics posts; other entries in the *Editorial Content Plan* would be your regular blog posts, topics to be covered, and brainstorming sessions with your Team on your posts.

24   Brainstorm with your Team:
Go here for 17 brainstorming resources you might use with your *Dream Team*:

http://onbloggingwell.com/17-blog-content-brainstorming-resources/#more-2583

25   Research other bloggers:
Research other blog posts. Select five competing authors (same genre) and follow their blogs. Give each post your own grade (0 = Blah, 5 = Very Good). Every 6 months, drop 2 authors and add 2 fresh ones, but once a year go back and recheck all those you are following.

If you are cooperating with other authors of the same genre (or are a member of one of the subtribes of Triberr), share your results with them so that you can all learn.

26   How to find blog ideas on Forums etc.:
Read forums and message boards (Google your book theme or proposed blog post topic and add the word *forum*

or *message board*), to find out what readers there are asking in their comments, and the forum topics.

Dip into everything you can access that deals with your book themes, such as magazines, and Facebook Pages dealing with topics matching your keywords and Author Brand.

Check this *brilliantbloggers* article for ideas on what to blog about:

http://www.blogworld.com/2011/09/29/44-brilliant-bloggers-talk-about-finding-post-ideas/

Forty four brilliant bloggers write about how they find ideas for blog posts.

One of the bloggers suggests writing a follow up post for your most popular post (a sequel); and expanding on an earlier How To post by picking one example and giving more detail.

For hints on how to write 500 word posts, read Judy Cullins' article here:

http://www.publishingbasics.com/2011/09/28/blog-marketing-how-to-write-500-word-posts-7-steps/

It's a very practical 7-step way to kick start your post by writing an outline with sub points, a few sentences for each sub point and then the full paragraphs for each sub point heading.

27   The Three Bites Rule: Multiple Uses:

Every post or item you create for promotion should be used at least 3 times in different ways.

The rule makes your ideas go further by calling for you to repackage ideas for a different purpose:

- You can change the type of promotion vehicle you use (convert a written blog post into a video);
- expand and widen a Facebook Page entry for use in a blog post along with a video;
- write prequels and sequels of your best ideas;
- add new material, that covers a trending topic, to an older post to give it a fresher and different slant; and
- revisit the better promotional messages in your posts for your 6-monthly *My Best Of Series* of blog posts.

28   Ask for ideas for Posts:

It's one way to engage them in your journey as a writer and member of the Indie Community.

Brainstorm how to ask them with your *Team*.

You might ask your readers to think about a named subject before giving you ideas for blog post topics, such as: what features of current events might appeal to your Personas, or how a member of the Indie Community can better promote her book.

Often you can find suggestions in the Forums.

Are there questions your Target Readers would like to be answered, that you could write about and your readers could comment on?

29   Great Graphics for your Author Blog:

Pictures are worth a thousand words, and good graphics liven up any blog post.

Choose good images for your posts (Google *public domain images* plus your topic to get images not subject to copyright, or use your own images).

Use a *caption* to link the image to your topic, and experiment with the different kinds of *borders* you can use for the images.

Use the tools on Blogger to upload images (the Add Image icon). You then Browse to the file on your computer, choose Layout and Size and then Upload.

TIP: I usually store images I intend using in my posts in a *Picture* subdirectory in my main Glenn Ashton Author bookmark directory. Another subdirectory contains *Raw Material* for later use, and the third one has *Draft Posts*.

This makes writing my blog much easier because I don't have to hunt for everything: it's all in one place.

30 Bullet your way to Successful Blogging:

Readers flit onto your blog, hover for a few seconds, and if nothing hooks them, they flit away, seeking some other place to land.

Your job is to hook them in three seconds. And if you confront them with poorly designed headlines and dense text in your post, they will flit away.

Keep them looking with a clean layout, a great image linked to the headline, and bullets instead of dense forests of text.

31 Secret of Success: Link! Link! Link!

Reciprocity is the name of the game when linking.

The unwritten law of the Indie Community is this: You link to me in your blog posts and I will link to you in mine.

You should also link to your *earlier posts* (on similar topics) so that your readers can read more of your posts. Use *Yet Another Related Post (YARP)* plugin for a Wordpress blog to do this, and *LinkWithin* for any Blogger post.

I use *hyperlinks* to my earlier posts: you highlight the text you want (I use words like *In my earlier post I discuss X*, and highlight these words) then click on the Link icon at the top of the page to go to the post you are linking to. It's very easy to use.

You can also link to other bloggers' posts; this adds value to your readers, gives you a smidgeon of authority by association, and might lead to them linking to your blog.

To attract other bloggers to link to your posts, you have to give them a reason to do so. Use *link magnets* (posts that other bloggers feel would add value to their own blogs); often the How To types of posts on popular topics, or very good videos, do the trick.

Check this *dummies.com* article on how to solicit unpaid links from another web site:

http://www.dummies.com/how-to/content/how-to-solicit-an-unpaid-link-from-another-web-sit.html

Some good hints there on how to approach other bloggers for reciprocal links.

If you are cooperating with other members of the Indie Community, speak to them about reciprocal linking.

32   Feedback and Good Blogging:

Always ask readers to comment on your blog posts. Never ask, never get!

The blogosphere is filled with the walking-dead blogs; the ones where the blog owner posts away, and nobody reads. These blogs are dead. Kaput. Pining for the Norwegian fjords.

Living blogs are easy to spot. They show signs of life.

There is no end to the type of feedback you can seek, just make it relevant to your blog post topic. Bounce some ideas off your Team about what kinds of feedback you could ask for.

Other Tips for your Author Blog:

33   *Twitter* –

Link your blog to your Twitter account (go to Settings then to Sharing in your blogger dashboard to do so).

34   *Newsletter* –

Use your blog to invite subscriptions to your regular, free e-newsletter. Publish one once a month (you can always go weekly if demand is there) and use the newsletter to engage your subscribers in more depth. You can also ask friendly Indie Community members to post articles on your e-newsletter.

35   *Social Network Editorial Calendar* –

Set one up as part of your Small Steps Plan. It makes preparing for future blog posts easier because you know what's coming down the road.

Here's one free template for a *Social Network Editorial Calendar* for you to download and consider using:

http://connect.slingshotseo.com/free-template-editorial-calendar

36   *Videos –*

Add your Author Videos and Book Videos to your blog (see Task 19). If you have a video camera take it with your everywhere just in case.

37   *Repeaters –*

<u>Repeat visitors and commentators are keys for your blog</u>. They are more engaged than the others, and so are prime targets for your reward plans.

Check if they have a Twitter account and send them their **Prized Commentator Award** you and your Team have designed, via Direct Message.

38   *Check your Me versus Others ratio –*

Be low key in blogging about yourself; blog about your themes, and third parties. Narcissistic bloggers often bore readers.

Work out a Me versus Others ratio for your blog posts topics (try 1:4 to start with) and see what happens to your blog visits if you experiment with a higher or lower ratio of posts.

Blog about the themes of your books rather than about the books themselves; your themes are more universal, less egocentric.

39   *Nuggets Reminder –*

Add a little section at the end of your blog posts under the heading Nuggets Reminder, and refer to topics, hints, points or references mentioned in your post, along with links to other sites mentioned. Don't overload this section, though.

40   *Capture your Indie Journey* –

Share your journey as a self-publishing author on Amazon and Kindle with your readers, through a series of posts on your Author Blog talking about what you are doing, what your plans are, how your plans are working out etc. Make it personal, make it interesting.

This site is an example from *absolutewrite.com*:

http://absolutewrite.com/forums/showthread.php?t=2 28048

41   *Blogger stats* –

Dip into your blogger stats from time to time. I check the popularity of various posts using it. Warning: it's addictive.

42   *Engagement* –

This article by Joel Friedlander on the CreateSpace Community gives some hints on upping the engagement level of your Author Blog:

https://www.createspace.com/en/community/docs/D OC-1501

He makes the point that those who comment on your blog posts are showing a willingness to enter into your conversation in public way, so target them and respond to encourage this continuing. *Repeat visitors are also on the higher level of the engagement scale.*

At the top of your engagement scale are those who subscribe to your blog (they join it to become followers). Subscription (to your blog, your newsletter) is a key indicator of interest.

He uses his *keywords* in his blog posts, and has found that these keywords do lead readers who search for them to his. He uses the *Google Adwords Keyword Tool* (Google it) to find keywords that fit his niche.

43   *Keywords* –

Use Google Adwords Keyword Tool to find keywords that fit your Author Brand, your book's genre and description, and are power words.

44   *Keyword phrases* –

Most people search using keyword phrases and not just single keywords. This article by *dummies.com* gives some hints on how to use keyword phrases so as to improve your blog's ability to be found in Google searches:

http://www.dummies.com/how-to/content/how-to-choose-effective-keyword-phrases-for-search.html

One hint is to use as many keywords about your blog post topic that you think people might search for in your posts.

And avoid general phrases as keywords, and use descriptive words as well.

45   *Rewards for Comments* –

Encourage comments on your blog posts by offering rewards.

Here's one example of such a reward:

"Post a comment below about this article or the Write to Win blog and get a chance to receive one of two FREE Book Writer's Success Kits I'm giving away throughout this week. Congratulations to Bonnie McDonald who won the last Success Kit."

Every now and then (start monthly?), reward people who comment on your blog posts by giving them a free eBook of yours, or other rewards. You will need them to provide an email address and name to qualify for the reward.

You might consider simply random gifts to commentators (once per month?).

Check for writers and bloggers in your niches on *Scribnia* and *Technorati*, to find some to follow and study; at these sites:

http://www.scribnia.com/

http://technorati.com/

You can visit the niche communities to seek inspiration for topics for your own Author Blog.

46 *Strike while the iron is hot with Trends*–

Check your topic or keywords on *Google Trends* and on *Google Hottrends* to find out what is trending, and try to *get in front of the curve* with a blog post on something similar. Check the Forecast box in Trends to see how the trend is expected to behave.

How can you relate the hottest trends to your book themes, your Author Brand, or the impact of those trends on your Target Readers Personas? Brainstorm this with your Team.

47 *Become a Prophet* –

Predict the future in some of your blog posts, if you have views about what might happen in areas covered by your Author Brand or book themes.

48   *Join the fight!* –

Join in controversies as part of your Author Blog posts, but don't go so far overboard you offend your readers.

Ask the dummies for ideas to blog about; find them here:

http://www.dummies.com/how-to/content/how-to-choose-what-to-blog-about.html

Follow your own interests and passions when choosing a topic to blog about.

49   *Don't write, talk!*

Don't *write* your blog posts, *have a conversation* with your Target Readers! Go for blogspeaking, not writing. Keep your Target Readers Personas firmly in mind as you start thinking about what to say in your blog post. *Talk* to them, don't write *at* them.

50   *Your Engagement Checklist* –

Get your Team to read your written Brand Touches (draft blog posts, Facebook entries, author and book videos, tweets, forum participation, your newsletter etc.) and then mark them, using the checklist headed *9 Engagement Tests of My Brand Touches.*

This test has 9 parts, as follows:

"9 Engagement Tests of My Brand Touches

Please rate the attached Brand Touch on the scale 0 to 5, with 0 = Boring and 5 = Very Good, in each of the 9 categories below, and add comments if you have any:

Author Brand: Is this consistent with my Author Brand?

Goals: Will it help to achieve the goals of my Small Steps Plan?

The Hook: Do the post heading and the opening sentence Hook the Target Readers? Why?

Engaging: Does it engage the reader intensely? Will it encourage comments?

Me: Does it make Me sound like an interesting person, worth following?

Tone: Does the tone fit the Target Readers Personas I am talking to?

Reader benefit: Does this benefit the reader in any clearly understood and compelling way? How?

Call to Action: Does it contain a call to action that is compelling?

Other comments: Please comment on anything else you feel I need to think about.

[Your Name]"

51 *Plan your Blog*:

Plan ahead for contents of your blog, to take pressure off and allow your creative juices to flow. Add the planning sessions to your Small Steps Plan Tasks; start with 3 future posts (later on, 5 and then 10).

52 **Guest Blogging: What is Guest Blogging?**

A guest blogger writes a blog post that is published by a second blogger on his or her own blog. You might be the guest, or you might be the host and invite other bloggers to contribute their posts to your Author Blog.

Your guest appearance might take the form of an *interview* of you by the publishing blogger, or vice-versa; or it might be a *post* on some topic you have chosen.

You aim is to spread knowledge of your own Author Brand to the readers of the blog that is your host blog.

53   What is a Blog Swap?

Another variation is a ***blog swap*** – you both write a post and you each publish the other's post on your blog. The topics of the posts might be the same, or they might be totally different. You could have a one-off blog swap, or a whole series of them, on one or more topics. Blog swaps might lead to the readers of the host blog deciding to follow the you because they liked your post.

Your aim is the same: name recognition and brand spreading.

Please help build the Indie Community by promoting blog swaps with other Indie members.

54   How do you start Guest Blogging in other blogs?

Add to *the **Editorial Content Plan*** portion of your Small Steps Plan regular contacts by you of other bloggers to be their guests on their blogs (and/or do a blog swap with them). Start with a monthly outreach target, and reduce it to at least one outreach per week as you get more comfortable with the concept of guest blogging.

Check Danny Iny's description of how he started being a guest blogger at:

http://writelikefreddy.com/site/about-danny-iny/

Dip into *Copyblogger* and *Problogger* – the two sites Danny refers to in his posts – for hints on what content is attractive. *Note that Danny also asked blogs that did not advertise that they would host guest bloggers, if he could provide them with a post.* If you like a blog, or find a blog with a lot of outreach, consider doing the same.

Some copies of his posts can be found here:

http://writelikefreddy.com/site/danny-guest-posts/

Google *guest blogging* for articles on it, and dip into Twitter – the hashtag is #guestblogging.

55   Your goals for Guest Blogging –

Before you start talking to other host blogs, do a bit of brainstorming with your Team on your goals with guest blogging. What are you trying to achieve? Keep these goals in mind when you talk to hosts.

Examples of such goals are:

- To increase my name recognition in [define the circles e.g.: writers of thrillers];
- to advertise my Author Brand;
- to work with the host blogger to see whether he or she could become a cooperative Indie Community member and do things together with me and others in my cooperation group;
- to invite the readers of the host blog to subscribe to my newsletter, etc.

56   Homework before Guest Blogging –

Read the posts on the blog you want to be your host, and understand the topics, the word counts, the use of images, headlines that hook, the structure of the posts, the way the host interacts with commentators, and the style of writing.

Before you approach the host to ask him to use your guest post, decide in detail what your post will be about, based on the research you have done. How can you add value to your host's blog with your post? If you can't pitch the host on what's in it for him or her, why should they ask you to be their guest?

Never go just cap in hand to a host blogger to ask to be the guest; always take an idea and a framework with you, to show you are serious.

57   Comments on your Guest Blog post –

If you get comments on your guest post, you must respond and join in the macrologue. That's an essential step to establish your Author Brand.

58   *Hints* for Guest Blogging –

Read the hints in *brilliantbloggers* (and the other articles linked to) to make sure you do this properly:

http://www.blogworld.com/2012/06/22/28-brilliant-bloggers-talk-about-guest-posts/

Doing your homework is necessary – it's called "blog scouting" in this article.

59   Invite Guest Bloggers to my own Blog?

I recommend that you add to your *Editorial Content Plan* a few dates for you to start a program of inviting guest blogs (especially Indie blogs) for your own blog. Check the *rules* that the best host blogs you come across use for their guests, and select those that appeal to you; this makes things clear to everyone what's needed.

More Tips for Guest Blogging:

60   Swaps –

Consider agreeing to swap guest posts on each other's blogs with other Indie bloggers. Agree the length, the topics and the timing, to avoid misunderstandings. All swappers should reserve the right not to publish any guest post for any reason.

61   Quotable quotes –

John Locke recommends something important:

"I recommend you develop at least one highly-quotable remark for each interview or guest blog, and that you go into the encounter with a theme, and pound that theme over and over."

So, write quotable quotes for your guest blogging interviews.

62   Interviews –

If you are going to be interviewed, or are going to do interviews of other bloggers for your own blog, then prepare your list of questions and facts beforehand so that you are ready.

Join the Brilliant Bloggers and do some guest blogging according to their schedule.

63   Make them curious –

Leave something in your guest post about yourself that hooks the readers and makes them want to tune into your own Author Blog to find out more about you and your books and the way you write.

64   Make them remember you –

When those readers finish your guest post, what have you done or said that makes them remember you, so that the next time they see your name they want to follow your own blog?

65   Don't keep the good ones –

Offer your best posts to host bloggers; don't try to fob them off with your second-rate ones. That way they are more likely to invite you back again. Read the article by Darren Rowse for more hints:

http://www.problogger.net/archives/2010/02/24/9-ways-become-an-exceptional-guest-poster/

I like his comments on using the right format, and on including links to other posts in the host blog in your guest post.

66   Fifty blog content ideas –

From *pumpupyourbook* comes a list of 50 topics you might use for your normal blog posts, or for your guest posts:

http://www.pumpupyourbook.com/2011/01/13/guest-posts-50-ideas-for-great-guest-posts-for-authors-on-virtual-book-tours/

Taking your Author Blog on Blog Tours:

67   What is a Blog Tour?

You can think of getting one of your own posts used as a guest post by another host blog as a kind of one-stop internet tour, as compared to a blog tour which involves your touring many blogs, with your guest posts appearing, or written or audio interviews of you by the host blogger, your author or book videos, or even reviews of your book by the host blogger.

You stay in one place, but your guest posts, interview or the reviews of your books etc. move around several blogs.

A blog tour usually takes place within a set timeframe, a week or a month.

Before you start your tour, you will have to a bit of planning. Are you going to offer guest posts, or interviews of you, or ask for reviews of your book, or all of these? You could let the host blogger decide.

Do you know how many blogs you want to tour? Have you done your research on these blogs?

Have you prepared your pitch to the hosts? Would it persuade you to host them?

Have you included the benefits they will get from your touring? How sharp are the hooks you included?

Have you prepared some guest posts in advance, or at least outlines of what they will be about?

I suggest you start with preparing for a smallish tour, with a handful of blogs, to get the hang of it, and work your way up to bigger tours (your small steps and small wins strategy).

Have you decided on your goals for the tour? Do so.

For the insights of 28 authors, read the article by Eric Van Der Hope:

http://www.blogworld.com/2012/06/22/28-brilliant-bloggers-talk-about-guest-posts/

Don't forget to offer to reciprocate any tour your hosts might make! And encourage your own readers to skip along to each stop on your tour to see your offerings.

68   Where can you find Blog Tours?

Google *how to find blog tours* and check out a few of the answers, such as this one:

http://www.blogtour.org/

Ask your readers for hints on the best places to find existing blog tours that you might join.

TIP: If you are cooperating with fellow Indie Community members, or your own Writers Club, perhaps you could organize a blog tour using your own group blogs as tour stops?

Explore the various forums that fit your book's genre, to find out what participants have written about blog tours.

69   How to prepare for your Blog Tours

Check out the samples of case histories at the *Patron Saints Productions* site:

http://www.patronsaintpr.com/

Read a few of them to get a feel for what is involved in any blog tour. Some of them are very interesting.

You will need to brush off your Book Elevator Speech and your Author Elevator Speech because you will be using it several times, both during your introduction to your blog tour appearances, and in answer to comments or questions.

Google *blog tours* and read a few to get a feel for what happens. Jot down notes in *My Bloggy Book* for your own future use.

70   Starting your own Blog Tour:

a. Step-by-step:

Joel Friedlander has a step-by-step process for organizing your blog tour in his article *Deskbound Destinations: Understanding Blog Tours*:

https://www.createspace.com/en/community/docs/DOC-1831

Note the advantages of a blog tour he spells out, and some concrete steps to take before and after the tour (I like the post-tour review).

b. *Two types of tours*:

You can organize two kinds of blog tours. You might opt for the blog tour where you do the touring, which means you have to find the tour hosts and provide them with your products.

Or you can help develop the Indie Community by (either alone or working with other cooperative Indie authors) setting up a blog tour and inviting other writers to attend the tour. You would be arranging the blog stops, and providing the products to be hosted at those blog stops. You might also go on the blog tour as an author, along with the other authors you have invited to join the tour and provide their products.

c. *How to invite bloggers to your own tour:*

For some hints on how to ask host bloggers to invite guest bloggers to your own tour, check this article by Tristan Higbee:

http://www.searchenginepeople.com/blog/how-to-invite-guest-blogger.html

He has four very good points (be flattering; explain the benefits; be specific about the topics you want your guests to write about; and make it as easy as possible for them).

TIP: Offer prizes of your eBook to randomly drawn commentators on any blog tour you either are a guest of or host of. Remember your three primary goals of your promotion plan. Consider asking the winners to do a blog-swap with you if the winner has her own blog, and always ask them to post a review of your eBook on Kindle.

d. *Preparing for your own blog tour:*

Check here for 28 questions from *pumpupyourbook* about your readiness for a virtual book tour:

http://www.pumpupyourbook.com/2012/01/13/pump -up-your-book%E2%80%99s-28-point-virtual-book-tour- checklist/

And from the same site, 10 reasons why virtual book tours make sense for authors:

http://www.pumpupyourbook.com/2011/08/16/10- things-you-need-to-know-about-virtual-book-tours/

Check *Kindleboards.com* to find authors who might be prepared to participate in your blog tour or guest posts or author interviews (see Task 7 for more on the Writer's Cafe and Kindleboards).

71   *Rating your author blog:*

Hubspot has a blog grader that might give you some tips:

https://marketing.grader.com/

1   What is Facebook?

Facebook is a social network that allows you to connect with friends and others.

You register and then set up your **Profile Page** and you are in business.

Finding friends is easy, as you can use your email address to do so, or search for them by name. You send the other person a Friend request, and if they agree, you are now Facebook **Friends** and can talk to each other.

You only interact with Friends, and they with you, but you should read the privacy rules carefully because friends of friends might also access all the information you place on Facebook.

Using Facebook costs you nothing (unless you start buying gadgets and other add-ons that are for sale).

2   Your Small Steps Plan to use Facebook:

You should have three primary goals in your Facebook Promotion Plan (Email, Joining, Converting).

Making yourself noticeable in a sea of one billion users seems hopeless, but your aims are much more modest to start.

You tailor your messages to appeal to your Target Readers.

TIP: You need to develop a *content strategy*, and the best way to do this is to add it to your **Editorial Content Plan**.

The comments made under your Author Blog in Task 5 about engaging your readers apply here, too.

Your Facebook friends also need to be *rewarded*, just as your interactive readers of your Author Blog do (see Task 5).

Dip into the article on *betsie's literary blog* entitled *How to Market a Novel* for 10 leading questions for targeting fiction readers for more hints on how to engage your Facebook fans; also found here:

http://betsie.tripod.com/literary/id76.html

3   How to start your Facebook page:

GCF LearnFree.org have a free tutorial for starting on Facebook entitled Facebook 101 that is worth going through; just Google *Facebook 101* or go here:

http://www.gcflearnfree.org/facebook101

When you register, you set up your **Profile**, which needs a personal picture. You don't have to add any personal information, and might not until you are very comfortable with Facebook.

Add photos to your **Album** (where you store photos others can see); your book, other images fitting your Author Brand; localities in your book etc.

Then you add known **Friends**, and start searching for others to add as Friends if they agree. The search option allows you to look for specific people you know, and also for profiles of people using word searches.

You can send **Messages** to your Friends; this is not email, and behaves more like a conversation between friends than an email. All your messages to a friend are in one place and you can see everything you said to that friend as if it was one long conversation between you.

Check the Facebook instructions for adding friends and sending messages; they are very clear and easy to apply.

Welcome to the *Facebook Wall*. It works just like a wall in a street, and is the place on everyone's profile where others can leave a *Note* (you will find the Note icon in many places). You can also add photos and videos and other media items on the Walls of others.

I think the Wall plus Messages are the two most effective features of Facebook for an author's Small Steps Plan.

4   Two Questions before you use Facebook:

You need to answer two major questions before your plunge into Facebook. First, who are your Target Readers? Review Task 3 above to answer this one. Second, what level of personal information do you want to allow people to view on Facebook, and why? Don't just answer all the questions you are asked when you register.

5   Type of Posts for your Facebook page?

The content of your Facebook posts will be partly determined by your *Editorial Content Plan*.

Dan Zarrella of *Hubspot* has done some research on more than 1.3 million posts to find methods to get more Likes and more Comments and more Shares on Facebook, and discovered the kinds of posts that attract the most Likes. Google *dan zarrella get more likes facebook* for the full article; there are others in his site worth reading. Consider his findings when deciding on posts, and follow his blog.

Here are some TIPS from Dan for you to consider:

- Posts with **photos** beat the spots off all other kinds of posts when it came to getting the Big 3 (Likes, Comments and Shares). For Shares, **videos** came next in line.

- Longer posts got shared more often, but very short or very long posts got more Likes. So vary the length of your posts to gain more Shares and more Likes.

- Want more Likes? Use the word **"I" and "me"** more in your posts; Facebook readers are OK with more narcissism than other social networks are. I guess Facebook is a more personal kind of social network.

- If the **tone** of your post is neutral, it will get fewer Likes.

- Follow Dan Zarrella's blog HubSpot's Inbound Marketing Blog for superb articles on marketing in cyberspace.

- **When to post?** Dan found that later in the day (eastern time) will get you more Likes and Shares (Shares peak around 6pm and Likes around 8pm). Posting on Saturday and Sunday will get you more Likes than during the week.

- **How often** should you post to get more Likes? Dan's finding was to post regularly, but not more than once per day and best of all once every day. More is not better on Facebook, it seems.

- Remember *Headlines that Hook* – in Task 5 above? Dan found a slight preference for sharing Facebook posts with a number (0 to 10) in its headline.

- Does **sex** sell? Posts on Facebook with headlines that were positive about sex were shared more.
- Use **simple language** if you want your posts shared more on Facebook – grade 9 or lower readability.
- What **words** in post titles lead to more shares? These: best, most, why and how. Geek alert - he also found which words were not good if you want more sharing.
- **Good news** or bad news? Both Twitter and Facebook readers find negative remarks a downer if you want your posts to be shared. The power of positive writing!
- And finally, read Dan Zarella's post *A Box of Crayons, Not a Rubber Stamp* for more words of wisdom on the need to make your social networks communal places, where people can participate and leave bits of themselves to add to the communal story.

Posts for your Clan members – Google *Amy Porterfield 9 facebook marketing strategies to build super fans* to check her hints for what you could post to engage your fans.

More TIPS on Promoting using Facebook:

6   **Use Events to get Likes on your Page:**

You can <u>create an event and invite your Facebook friends to join the event</u>.

You host the event and can choose different privacy setting for who can see or join or add guests to your event. Group members can also arrange events that appear on the group's Wall and members may choose to join the event. Ask people to Like your Page in return for being invited to your Event.

If you are a member of a Writers' Club you can arrange a joint Event, hosted by you or by some other member, which allows you to cooperate with say 4 other authors to give out free eBooks to guests. Google *Facebook Event to Help Multiple Indie Authors* for some hints.

You use Events to keep fans updated with snippets about your next novels, your journey as author, contests etc. It is available from the apps menu bar on the left of your Facebook home page. You input the event name, the time and date, its description, a photo if you wish, and invite guests from your friends.

7   Add a Forum to your Facebook Page:

The discussion boards were ended on Facebook, but you can add a forum to your Page - Google *forumforpages* for details. You can add a *new topic* by clicking on that, or go to *forum settings* at the bottom left to customize your forum settings.

Check this as well:

http://www.wikihow.com/Create-a-Forum-on-Facebook-with-FacebookForums.net

Google *facebook author forums* and browse the results for hints on Facebook forums of other authors you could join, or on topics or layouts you could use in your own Facebook forum.

8   How to move your Blog posts to your Page:

RSS Graffiti is a service that automatically <u>moves posts from your blog and news sources to your Facebook profile</u>, page, group or wall. It started in 2009 and is now used by over a million people. It is a free service. Google *rss graffiti* for more details.

More TIPS to use Facebook in your Plan:

9   *Authors on Facebook* –

Google *authors on facebook list* to find details and then send friend requests to those you want to smooze with.

10   *Likes* –

The most powerful feature of Facebook (apart from photos and messages), is the ability of any person reading your Facebook page to click Like under the entry; this might encourage others to check it out. Your aim is to gather as many Likes for your Author Blog posts and book items as you can, hoping that others will follow and read.

But don't hold your breath: many people do drive-by Likes without too much thought.

11   *Your Book Page* –

You should read how to set up a Page for your book on Facebook (under the Artist, Band or Public Figure group-ing, subgroup Author, then go to Entertainment and on to Book). What is a Page? Think of it as a sub-website within Facebook that holds information; and allows Likes to be added. Your followers on your Book Page are called **Fans** (**Friends** are followers on your Profile Page). You are allowed more than one page, so think about an **Author Page** as well.

12 *Insights* –

Check these every now and then; it is an analysis age, sex and location of people who Liked your Book Page.

13 *Paid advertising* –

Once your Promotion Plan is up and running, check out the paid advertising possibilities Facebook offers.

14 *Getting followers* –

Read Emily Chand's February 2011 article *Build a Facebook author page and get people to "like" it: a 20-step guide* for some ideas (Google it to find it).

Read about how to use **Events** to ask people to Like your book page; and adding **RSS Graffiti** also from the Apps group; and finally about adding a **discussion board** to your Book Page from the Apps group.

15 *Link* –

Link your Facebook page to your other social networks by adding a Like Me button to the sidebar of your Author Blog and Twitter profile.

16 *Keywords* –

Scatter them on your Fan Pages but don't overdo it so stick to the top 5 or so.

17 *Calls to Action* –

Add them to your post updates so that people will share your post with their friends and so increase your outreach.

18   *Good Fan Pages* –

Google *incomediary* and *20 best designed facebook fan pages* for examples (with commentary) of one person's selection of well-designed fan pages. Bob Marley's call to action to *join a movement* is an interesting alternative to a plain Like plea. Why not use *Click to support the Indie self-publishers* on your page?

19   *Continuous Improvement* –

Once you are up and running, add as a Task to your Small Steps Plan improvements of your Facebook presence; Google *how to make good facebook fan pages* for hints.

20   *Your own Character Pages* –

Which character(s) in your book could do with their own Page? How could you make posts to this page meet the 3 social network needs of your Target Readers? How about starring your villain in his or her own Page?

21   *Indie Community Page* –

Would you like to add a Page that supports self-published authors on Amazon and Kindle? Or the Indie Movement more generally?

What kind of posts would that open up for you?

Could you add Calls to Action which would allow your readers to boost other self-published writers?

How about asking readers to drop into your random choices of Indie author blogs? Pages can work well for movements, especially if you connect them to Affinity

Groups related to your book's theme (see Task 3 above on such groups).

22   *More hints* –

Google *dummies.com how to set up your facebook page* and check out the hints about what to put in your page in the 10 posts in this series.

23   *Engage your Fans* –

Ask them for their take on your topic; thank them for commenting etc.; share you insights – remember their 3 needs from social networks: they want to be entertained; they want to find things to send to their own friends so that they are entertained; or they want to learn something (either for their own sake, or to stay current in their social interactions).

24   *Fan of the Month (FOTM)* –

Once you have enough Fans, start your own Fan of the Month celebration and post about the chosen Fan, their successes, etc. Interview them and ask for a photo to add to your post. You can select a random FOTM based on their activity (Likes, Comments, Shares).

Or else you might poll your readers to select the winner.

Give all entrants free copies of your eBook (up to a maximum); or name a character in your next book after them. Google fan of the month for ideas about how others run such contests. Check how Authors Love Readers run their collective Fans of the Month posts. Should you do the same with other authors?

25   *Author Fan Pages* –

Google *author facebook fan page* to see how other authors have set up their own fan pages.

26   *Custom Facebook Lists* –

Use the Lists feature to share a post with your hand-picked audience or to exclude others from a post.

You choose whether to share or hide content with one of more lists using the audience selector.

Lists is on the left-column of your Facebook home page.

27   *Engage through Polls* –

Use public polls like *polldaddy.com* to engage your readers with polls you design.

Wrap the polls around your book's theme or topics from it, or characters.

Or create lively, unusual quizzes that fit your Author Brand but stand out, or are topical, or promote the Indie Community in vivid ways.

28   *Contests* –

Read how to set up promotions on Facebook that fit their rules by Googling *dummies.com how to create facebook promotion.*

Hints include running it for one month; keeping it simple; cross-promoting on your other social networks; and making it uniquely you.

29   *Notes* –

Do add **photos** to your notes if they fit the topic.

30   *Tags* –

If you mention your **friends** in your Notes, tag them by typing the @ sign before their name; you choose the right person from the menu that appears.

31   *Photo contests* –

Run one from your Facebook page but stick to the rules re promotions.

32   *Become a Facebook Groupmeister* –

A powerful Facebook tool for self-published authors is the ability to form Groups.

The left column of your home page has Create Group. You give your group a name, add members and decide on the privacy setting for your group.

Groups let you create a private space, which you can share with a small group of people.

You can post updates, chat with everyone at once, poll your group.

You decide who shares in what by creating different groups.

You have 3 types –

- a secret group means only group members see what other members post;
- a closed group means anyone can see the group and who is in it, but only members see the posts; and
- an open or public group means anyone can see the group and who is in it and also what members post.

Be creative when forming groups; brainstorm possible groups with your Team.

Here are some ideas for you to discuss with your Team:

- Think about a group for your Writers' Club.
- What about a group for your Clan of Supporters, who share in the makings of your next novel? Or in advising you on your planned promotion messages?
- Another secret group for your Brand Ambassadors to exchange views on your promotions, and an open group for your Brand Ambassadors which you use to thank them etc.?
- You can narrow the scope of your promotion messages by forming specific groups for specific purposes. Think about your book's genre, topics, themes, characters, localities: any ideas come to you for special groups wrapped around these?
- Perhaps form secret groups of your Personas which your Target Readers can join if they feel they fit into one of your Persona definitions; they can talk about what meets their needs etc., with you as host?
- Ask your Brand Ambassadors if any of them are willing to join your open group which allows anyone to ask for advice or offer advice on how to help Indie self-published authors, with you as host?
- How about forming a secret group of authors who are using the *Small Steps to Bigger Book Sales* promotional plan (invite me to join it, pretty please?)?

TIP: Research other Groups to get ideas for your own groups.

33 *Make regular status updates* –

It is your way to update others on your journey as an Indie author. Update your Profile, Facebook page and Group regularly; you can use photos or videos in an update. Your updates appear in the news feeds under the home tab in your profile. Friends can click Like or comment on your updates.

34 *More engagement* –

Google *how to make facebook page more engaging* and browse through the lists to see if any ideas make sense for your Page.

TIP: One of your Tasks in your Small Steps Plan should include periodically scanning the Internet to find similar articles, because new ideas keep popping up.

35 *Turn your Friends into Scouts* –

Invite your friends through posts on your Facebook forum to scan the Internet for you and find out the best ways used by authors to engage their fans on Facebook, through their blogs, on Twitter, and to report back to your private forum on their findings. Acknowledge those who do, thank them, and offer gifts (your free eBooks) to random draws of responders.

1   What are Internet Forums?

What is a Forum? <u>It is an online discussion site that has conversations posted to it as messages.</u>

Some forums require the messages to be vetted by a moderator before they are posted.

Single conversations on a forum are called *threads*. Some forums require all users to be registered if they wish to enter the conversations, while others allow anonymous comments.

Most forums allow people to read the conversations without having to log in to the forum.

Think of a forum as a public meeting place, located in cyberspace, in which everyone throughout the world with Internet access can join the conversation.

Sometimes called communities, they are also called discussion groups.

2   What about You & Forums?

Your challenge is to reduce the perceived risks of potential readers in buying your books. This risk arises because you are not a best-selling author, and thus a known commodity to potential readers.

The Amazon, Kindle and other communities or forums are essential channels for you to reduce these risks.

Also, the discussion boards on the many forums serve as magnets for readers looking for something new to read.

And they cost you nothing to join!

3   Amazon Communities & Boards:

The Amazon, CreateSpace and Kindle promotional tools (including the Amazon forums and Kindleboard) are the most powerful ones open to you as a self-published author. That's why the Amazon and Kindle promotion plans are the furniture on the first floor of your Author Platform Home. Making full use of these Amazon, CreateSpace and Kindle tools must be one of the earlier Tasks in your Small Steps Plan.

4   What are Amazon & CreateSpace communities?

Amazon communities are groups of readers who gather together to discuss things they are interested in, to post their own views on the topics, and to reply to comments made by others.

Discussions on such internet communities are also called *threads,* and they are shown as a list of messages and replies. Posts are also called messages.

Check this *Assisting Authors Online* site for a discussion of how to use Amazon communities to promote your book:

http://www.assistingauthors.com/2010/5-ways-promote-book-amazon-day-4-amazon-groups/

Amazon groups or communities are a vital part of the Indie Community and need your efforts to develop as a mutual help destination for writers.

The ***CreateSpace   Community   Discussion Boards*** are also very important gathering places for you in your plan to promote your own books.

They were set up by Amazon / CreateSpace to provide their author stable with a friendly environment, where they could talk about their own books (from writing it to marketing it) with others who have been through the same experience.

It is an exchange place for information, hints and help, as well as a powerful support for new authors. You find that site here:

https://www.createspace.com/en/community/community

Note the https (with an s) when you input the above address into Google.

5   Why are Amazon communities important to you?

Amazon is by far the largest online seller of books. And the Amazon and Kindle communities are sophisticated tools provided by them to help their authors to connect with other writers, and to succeed in their marketing of their books.

Their discussion boards serve as magnets for readers looking for something new to read, so you should think of them as **honeypots**, set up in trees by Amazon and Kindle, to attract bees (readers).

They are a source of therapy, inspiration, and advice from others in the publishing world, and are essential building blocks in the Indie Community.

TIP: Check out the reader-bees buzzing around the free honeypots set up in their community and discussion board trees by Amazon, CreateSpace and Kindle, as often as you can. Make them your second home!

Participate or die. But obey the rules! If you and your group of mutual-help Indie Community authors decide to help each other, do so within the rules of these communities.

Being a wallflower gets you nowhere in these communities; you have to participate (write comments, ask questions, post your own discussion threads, give advice etc.) Your Small Steps Plan simply has to include regular, quality participation by you in these communities. No ifs or buts. Just do it.

6   What Rules apply?

You can find the rules on each site.

You should read them carefully, because your participation will be monitored and steps taken against you if you do not. The rules are designed to prevent the dreaded *spamming*, and to enhance the quality of the sites.

Here are the CreateSpace guidelines, as an example:

https://www.createspace.com/Help/Community/Guidelines.jsp

You should pay particular attention to the rules prohibiting the advertising of your own books, or *self-promotion*.

Provide posts or comments that *add value* to the ongoing discussion on the community boards or discussion.

Stay on-topic in each thread; open another thread or find the right one if you want to talk about another topic.

Posts are welcomed on relevant experiences, ideas for new features, challenging questions, honest and supportive feedback.

Note when a link to your public Preview is allowed in your posts, as well as your author picture and links to external websites and images relevant to the topics.

These communities are important sources of your Target Readers and your Clan of Followers.

Note especially this CreateSpace guideline permitting certain posts which you should use:

Posts announcing or requesting feedback on a book, DVD or CD project created through CreateSpace. Limit the promotion of your CreateSpace project to one thread in the *Share Your Work* discussion board.

7   How to find Amazon Communities

Click here to go to the launching site of the Amazon communities:

http://www.amazon.com/gp/help/customer/display.html?nodeId=200280960

This Amazon guide to finding communities appears on the above page:

"Here's how you can find Customer Communities on Amazon.com and get back to those that you find to be interesting:

Most popular Customer Communities:

The Amazon.com tag cloud page shows the most popular topics of all time.

On every product page:

Customer Communities are featured on each product page. Scroll down below the Customer Reviews section and you will find a number of communities that are most relevant to the featured product.

Search for communities:

You can search Amazon.com for communities the same way you search for products. **The important difference is that you need to type in the topic followed by the word "community."** For example, try a search for *horror community* or *xbox 360 community*. If the community exists, it should be the first result you see, with a link to its discussion forum.

Jump directly to a community:

Advanced users can jump directly to the one community they want. The URL format is:

http://www.amazon.com/tag/foo where "*foo*" is the name of the community.

Examples: www.amazon.com/tag/science fiction and www.amazon.com/tag/wii."

You should use the Tag/foo Route to find Communities:

The easiest way to find any Amazon Community is to use the tag/foo route, where *foo* is the name of the community e.g.: www.amazon.com/tag/horror

Try it using your own genre and subgenres.

Or use the Amazon Search Route for Communities:

If you use the *Amazon search bar* on the Amazon.com site to find communities, just type in the topic and add the word *community*.

Example: use *science fiction community* not just *science fiction*.

8   Give Amazon Feedback on discussion boards:

The *Amazon Discussion Feedback Forum* (Google it for information) gives customers a place to provide feedback to Amazon on what they like or dislike about Amazon's discussion boards.

You should help develop the Indie Community by contributing any comments or hints you might have on the discussion boards / communities, to Amazon through this site (the design of the boards, the rules, ease of use, suggestions for improvements, who they would benefit, what Indie authors need from the discussion boards, new ways the boards could increase sales of Indie books, and why the feedback would work etc.).

9   Find hints for your Small Steps Plan in Customer Discussions:

Product pages have a heading *Customer Discussions*, which list the most recent and active discussions on that product; you can click on *See all discussions* to read all of them.

TIP: Browse through all the *Customer Discussions* on a particular product (e.g.: book of your competitor) on the product page to get a feel for how and what others discuss books. Make notes about the best entries in your ***My Bloggy Book*** for future guidance.

10   Plan your new topics for the boards / communities:

You should plan new topics that you can begin on the Discussions, dealing with items that allow you to make comments on your book themes etc. in a subtle way.

Starting a new topic is a one-click process on any Discussion page: you start one below the list of recently-active discussion titles by clicking on the discussion topic text box and then entering the initial post in the box that appears.

11   Ask for Email updates of boards:

You should also request email updates when new posts are made to discussions you have participated in. This helpful feature allows you to read the new posts and make new ones if you wish to. You should ask for email updates on all discussions you like.

12   How to Participate in Discussions:

Here are some hints about you and Discussions, from Maine Larry Crane:

http://mainelarrycrane.blogspot.ca/2012/09/how-to-participate-in-amazons.html

13   Amazon Book Forum:

Google *amazon book forum* and bookmark this site. Dip into it and comment on books you have read – especially those written by other Indie publishers, or by readers who are commenting on your own blog etc. No spamming your own books here, though! Add comments on this site to your tasks in your Small Steps Plan. It gets your own name out there: but make sure you add thoughtful value to the discussions.

14   Kindle Book Corner:

Google kindle book corner and bookmark the site; also provide comments and start new threads with topics of your choice, to get your name out there. Include this task in your Small Steps Plan.

1   What is Google+?

Google+ is a powerful new platform for writers (and others). It has a secret weapon that you can use to widen your network: you can organize your friends into **Circles**, and then decide exactly how much information you wish to share with each circle.

Launched in 2011 to compete with Facebook, Google + is a social networking service, owned by Google. It has more than 1.5 billion users, with just over one-third active users. So it is huge!

In Google+ you will find **Circles** and **Hangouts** (see below). Facebook has more than a billion users, and they spend far more time on Facebook than users do on Google+.

You can create your own conversations using the *Google+ Communities* feature, based on your choice of topic.

TIP: Google *googleplusdaily 10 things to do after joining google+* for some very good ideas of how you can use Google+ as a writer.

Bookmark *googleplusdaily* and add as a task in your Small Steps Plan periodically dipping into this site to see what latest developments you can use to promote your books.

2   How do you join Google+?
Google *google+* to go to the site. Sign in.

TIP: Get the *Mashable Beginner's Guide* by Googling *Google+ Communities: A Beginner's Guide* for a very good introduction to the social network site.

3 What does Google+ mean for writers?

Google *google+ and writers* for a slew of articles on how you as a writer may be able to harness the power of Google+ to your Indie carriage, and ride off into the sunset.

TIP: Consider starting your own Community on Google+ as a collaborative effort with your own Writers Club and/or with those in your Clan who are also authors; this shares the burden, adds freshness and other viewpoints; benefits all the members; and boosts the Indie Community.

4 Google+ Hangouts:

The powerful *Hangout* feature can be used by authors in many ways (see below for more discussion):

- You can Hangout with your Team.
- You can Hangout with your own Writers Club members.
- You can Hangout with those readers who have joined your Clan of Followers (but only in groups of 10 participants, including you as the leader, although unlimited others can watch it without participating).
- You can Hangout with your Brand Ambassadors.
- You can Hangout with selected readers who signed up for a Hangout with you on a chosen event.

5   Your Google+ Profile Pic:

One good thing to do is to have your ***Google+ profile picture*** shown in the Google results whenever a Google search throws up your blog posts. Read this article for the steps to do this: Google *Claim Authorship to Get Your Profile Picture in Google Results.*

6   Use Google+ Ripples to find Influencers and then ride their Ripples:

a. *What is Google+ Ripple?*

It is an diagram you can interact with that shows how a Google+ post ripples (or spreads) as it is shared by users.

So you can now follow any interesting post or person on Google+ and explore what happens in the Google+ universe.

Better still, Ripples shows the spreading of a hot post in real time! Warning: Ripples can become addictive.

b. *What do you see in a Ripple? –*

The person who made the first post on Google+ is shown in the center of a circle. If another user shares this post with others, through posts of their own, there are more circles, with those users in the center of their circles. You can end up seeing hundreds of circles all linked back to the one original post.

Google *ripples google* for a description of the Google+ Ripples program. It gives you an interactive graphic of the public shares of a URL or public post, that shows how it has rippled through the network.

It can be used to discover new and interesting people you might wish to follow.

You will see who has publicly shared the URL or post and their comments, how the post or URL was shared over time and statistics on the sharing.

You can add these people directly to your own Circles from the Ripple diagram; they have to agree to being enCircled, of course, for this to take. It takes two to Circle...

TIP: Google *Using Google+ Ripples to Connect with Influencers* for a very good explanation by SEOMoz of The Daily SEO Blog of how you can use Ripples to trace Influencers and increase your own reach.

c. *The Ripples diagram* –

To see the Ripples of a public post by someone on Google+ you simply click on the little arrow inside the circle on the right hand side of each post; the drop down menu includes the word Ripples. Click Ripples and you will see a diagram with circles and links – the Ripples.

• *Exploring the Ripples* –

Click on the diagram and dive deeper into the Ripples. You can then follow the posts of people who are in the Ripples diagram, to see who they are and what is on their Google+ site.

Play with them a bit until you are comfortable with splashing around in the Ripple pool.

Note that you are given a chance to add those people to your Circles (they have to agree to that before you both are enCircled).

d. *Riding the Ripples* –

So what can you do with Ripples? You can try to ride the Ripples of the most influential sharers. You can find connectors or influencers. You check what kind of content the influencer (someone with lots of Ripples) is sharing. Then follow such a shared post with Ripple to see where the post came from. You might then reach out to them to see if they will share your content.

Your aim is to have influencers (who have wide Ripples), sharing your content because this means a wider distribution of your posts. In other words, you try to ride their ripples to greater visibility.

Google *googleplusdaily ripples explained* for a very good analysis of the statistics you can research in your search for Influencers.

e. *Spreading Ripples* –

If you like the Ripples diagram of someone, share it with others by copying the URL of the Ripple and sharing that in your Stream.

TIP: *Splashing in the Ripples* - Add as a task in your Small Steps Plan diving into the Ripples of other authors and your readers, seeking Influencers to add to your Circles.

7   **Google+ Circles:**

Your *Circles* let you organize your groups so that you can share information with them.

You can hide who is in your Circles.

You can ask someone to join your Circle, but they have to agree and to include you in one of their Circles before it works.

Remember: two Circles make a connection, while only one Circle leads to emptiness.

You start off with the default list of Circles: Friends, Family, Acquaintances and Following, but you can rename them at any time.

TIP: *Circles growth* - Add as a task to your Small Steps Plan the adding of more and more Circles so as to make them ever larger.

a. *Segmenting with Circles* –

Circles is a powerful way to segment your target markets: by being very narrow in your list of Circles, you can have people that you can send very customized messages (content) to. So brainstorm with your Team what type of Circles you should form, and then feed those Circles with quality content.

b. *Google+ Stream* -

The Google+ **Stream** is the middle of the 3 columns on Google+ and this is where you will see updates from those users in your Circles.

You can decide whose posts you want to see in your Stream.

c. *Using your Circles* -

Circles is an easy way to share things with your friends, family, acquaintances, members of your Writers Club, book club members, members of your Clan of Followers, your Brand Ambassadors, members of the Indie Community, and anyone else you can think of.

TIP: ***Polish your Circles*** – If someone joins with you in a Circle, then reciprocate by reading their posts, engaging in conversations with them by sharing their posts with others, or commenting on them. Polish those Circles.

Sharing with your Circles is a win-win proposition: your post gets a wider circulation (good for your Author Brand visibility), while the other person who shared it with their friends and Circles meets one of their social networking needs by providing good content to their Circle. This increases the chances of her posts being shared in turn.

Your Google+ Page is very, very easy to share. This means the chances of your posts being shared are pretty high, *if you have value-added content on your Page*, and are seen as a contributor to the world of Circles (someone who gives and not just a taker).

TIP: ***Share with your Circles*** – Add as tasks to your Small Steps Plan, the sharing of posts by those swimming in your Stream.

8   Google+ Hangouts:

Another powerful program from Google+ that is going to revolutionize how Indies promote themselves and their books. You simply must become a Hangout expert; the more you do, the more you will learn and the more seasoned promoter you will become.

Hangouts is a free video conferencing tool.

Add as t*asks* to your Small Steps Plan your hosting several Hangouts and Hangouts on the Air over the next few months.

A Hangout is just that: you can hang out with other Google+ users, up to 10 in all at any time, and have video chat with each other.

You can also join in watching a YouTube video together in your Hangout.

All Hangout participants have to have a Google+ account.

Google *how to use google hangouts* for information on how to start.

You invite people to join your Hangout and they get a post on their Home page telling them they've been invited to join you, plus a list of the people in the Hangout at the time. They can decide to join your Hangout.

9   *Google Hangouts on Air* -

The new feature is *Google Hangouts on Air* (Google *hangouts on air* for their site), which allows you to videotape your Hangout of up to 10 people and have it broadcast for free on Google+, your YouTube channel, and your website that has embedded it.

Google *hangouts on air common questions* for more details of how to set up your own Hangouts on Air.

You won't need any special software, because your Hangout on Air is automatically saved to your YouTube account. You share your YouTube URL with those you invite to join you.

Although your Hangout is limited to 10 people, once you use Hangout on Air your Hangout session will be

<u>viewable by the public</u>; a counter on top of your Hangout window will show you how many are watching it.

You can edit your Hangout on the Air using your YouTube Video Manager, and this will automatically update your post.

10   *How can you use Hangouts on Air?*

Think of it as a free chance for you to use <u>your very own television show</u>, open to the whole wide world, to send out your messages as planned in your Small Steps Plan. Brainstorm with your Team how to use it. Here are some suggestions:

1. You can invite your Clan of Followers to join you in a discussion of your book, or of their views of self-published eBooks or any other topic that meets the 3 needs of social network users (because it entertains them, or helps them nurture their friends, or helps them to learn).

2. You can invite your Clan to view a working session of you and your handpicked Team.

3. You can air a discussion of aspects of writing you and your Writers Club are having.

4. You can launch a collective search with your Clan and your own Writers Club for videos and tutorials on how to write or books or self-promotion for Indie writers, and then watch them with your Hangouts and Circles.

5. You can get someone with a lovely voice and expressive features to read an extract of your book. Better still, you and someone else can play the part of characters in your book – think

engagement: ask your Clan members to join you in doing so.

6. Use Hangouts to make a virtual appearance before members of Book Clubs to promote your Author Brand and your books.

7. Why not rehearse with some Clan members and have them act as characters in your book, while you lob pointed questions at the characters?

8. Interview interesting people in the Indie Community and air the sessions.

9. Use Hangouts on Air to broadcast your own webinars.

10. Give your viewers a chance to see you writing a scene, with snippets of you at your desk, you talking to your Team about a character or plotline, you preparing messages for your Personas (with photos of each Persona and potted bios); drafts of your work, showing your revisions and explaining why you changed things; sessions discussing your research into topics and events for your next novel; chat with your Clan etc.

For more information on Hangouts, Google *25 brilliant bloggers talk about google hangouts*. Among the hints:

- promote your Hangouts on the Air well before show time;
- let them know their local time your show will appear;
- Google *Hangout Lower Third* for an app that shows your name and blog site on the bottom of your Hangouts on Air;

- don't forget to do your homework by prepping your guests you are going to interview;
- link up with your guests about half an hour before the show to make sure all the bugs are worked out before you go live;
- prepare a list of questions in case conversation flags;
- re-introduce guests during the show to make sure newcomers are up to date;
- ask viewers to +1, or share and to spread the word about your show; and
- offer to Hangout with other writers or readers on their Hangouts.

11   Google+ Promotional Tools for Writers:

Google *promotional tools for writers on google+ jason boog* for an article with some hints.

12   How (virtual and real) Book Clubs can use Google+ Hangouts:

Book clubs (or book clubs you and your Writers Club establish yourselves, by inviting your Target Readers to join your book club) can easily share conversations about books through using Google+ Hangouts, up to 10 at a time.

Google *how to use google+ hangouts jason boog* for a short article on how to do this.

You might want to gift your Kindle eBook to the members of the Book Club to entice them to join your own virtual Book Club; just make sure they fill in the sign up form so that they join your email subscriber list and you can send them your Newsletters (see Task 11).

Consider boosting the Indie Community by sharing details of your own Book Clubs with other Indie writers, so that your Book Club members may also read and discuss the books of those other self-published authors. Of course, you would expect (and ask) those other Indie authors to do the same for your eBooks with their own Book Clubs.

TIP: *Book Clubs & the 3 Bites Rule* – Once you have formed your own Book Club or two, write a post about how to do this and how to use Hangouts, for your Author Blog.

Because you can form virtual Book Clubs of your own (limited to 10 members per Circle), consider reaching out into *affinity groups* throughout the world to put together special virtual book clubs built around your Author Brand, your book's themes and characters, localities, and any other creative links you and your Team and Clan can think of.

13   How to share books on Google+:

Google eBooks can be shared with others on Google+ by clicking on the Google+ Share box on the About the Book page or in Google Books preview.

You simply add your message, select the lucky Circles you are sending the suggestion to, and click *share*. The book cover plus your message then floats into your Google+ Stream.

TIP: *Circles, You and Google eBooks* – Consider forming special Circles from your readers who are interested in sharing good Google eBooks, and then share them with the Circle via the Share feature of Google+

14   **Authors and Writers on Google+:**

One fruitful source for populating your Circles is to find authors who are on Google+ and wish to connect with other writers.

TIP: *You & Writers on Google+ - Google writers on google+ jason boog* and bookmark the site, which has a list of writers who want to connect with other writers on Google+

TIP: *Google+ Writers* – Add as tasks to your Small Steps Plan reviewing the writers who want to connect with other writers in the post *Writers on Google+* by Jason Boog and adding some of them to your own Circles, so as to boost authors in general and the Indie Community in particular.

Google *list of recommended authors on google+* for another list of writers to consider adding to your own Circles and belonging to theirs.

1   What is Pinterest?

A must for you as an Indie publisher.

Pinterest is <u>an online pin board (a virtual corkboard)</u> that lets you organize and share anything you want.

You email them and they invite you to join it. It is a free service. Check out the Wikipedia pinterest article for details – the story of how Ben Silbermann founded it is interesting: talk about an ability to promote!

The site's mission? To connect everyone in the whole wide world through the things they find interesting.

Think Facebook and Twitter, then think pictures: that's Pinterest. And how many words is a picture worth?

Note that over 60% of book buyers are women, and Pinterest is very, very popular with women (over 90% of the Facebook Likes for Pinterest come from women).

2   How big is Pinterest?

Pinterest is huge! More than 70 million users, more than 2 billion page views per month, and 5 million pins per day. That is a market you just cannot ignore. Users spend more time on Pinterest than they do on Facebook visits, according to one study.

3   Who uses Pinterest?

Match these statistics against your Personas. A 2012 study by MGAdvertising entitled Pin it to Win it showed women (87%) outnumbered men (13%). By age group: 3% in 0-17 years; 6% in 18-24; 27% in 25-34; 29% in 35-44; 24% in 45-54; the rest older.

Most USA users are women who are interested in hobbies, crafts, fashion, interior design, services, gifts and special events items.

4   How can a writer use Pinterest?

You should brainstorm how to use Pinterest with your Team, and with your Target Readers. Pinteresters often have themed boards, and delight in populating them with media they find online. It's easy to go forth and Pinterest, because all you do is use the *Pin It* button and voila! your board is populated.

Think **Linkage, Linkage, Linkage**! You are looking for the most arresting ways to link the themes of your promotional messages to images, and then to have others on Pinterest love them so much they spread them further and further, <u>with *your links to your landing pad (your Author Blog)* attached to them</u>.

Think of your keywords, your book's genre, your cover, your characters, the localities in your book, the themes in your book, the likes and dislikes, challenges and victories of all your Target Reader Personas, and come up with themes for boards.

Go through your Small Steps Plan goals, and your **Editorial Content Plan**, to match images you have found or made, to these, then sprinkle them with surrounding text, match them against your Author Brand to make sure they fit, and Pin them.

Add as t*asks* to your Small Steps Plan the adding of images to your Pinterest boards.

Use your **Author Videos** and **Book Videos** (see Task 19) for your Pinterest boards.

Google *pinterest for authors* for articles on how some authors use Pinterest. Jot down how they use Pinterest and the kinds of boards they have, in your *My Bloggy Book* for later use.

5   *Pinterest Boards* –

Find Pinterest boards you like, and *follow* them on Pinterest.

Ask your readers of your posts in your Author Blog and on your Facebook page to follow your Pinterest boards. The Pin Feed shows you the activity on the boards that you are following.

Google *public domain images* plus your topic, for copyright free images you can use. There are millions of them out there.

Remember: if you add value to people with your Pinterest items, they will be passed on, and your subtle promotional messages along with them. So think value and images. Can you get striking images to carry your value-added items (hints to solve problems, how-to articles or lists etc.).

6   *Your Book Characters* –

Think about the characters in your book. Can they support a Pinterest board of their own? The upbringing, character, education, age group, hobbies, interests, activities, conversations with them, extracts of dialogue from your book? How can you give them Hooks?

7   *Your Target Readers* –

Can you engage your Target Readers by having them pin items to your boards?

And then have the pins judged with prizes (your free eBooks? Your specially prepared rewards?) for the winners? How can you combine this with your email signup form to gain email addresses for your Newsletters?

What about a board for each of your books? The cover, the extracts, pics of places and events, videos of your chosen actors acting scenes from your book?

Make sure your pins of your book covers etc. link back to your Author Blog or to your Amazon Author Central page, so that they can buy the book if they fell in love with it via Pinterest.

Google *directory of book bloggers on pinterest* for a list of them at the *well read wife* blog.

8   *Tags* –

Your friends can tag your books by adding in your description "@TheirPinterestName".

9   *Your Indie Journey & Pinterest Board* –

Don't forget a few Pinterest boards dealing with your Journey as an Indie author.

Let them get to know you through your Pinterest story plus images. And all with links to your social network promotion channels (blog, twitter, Facebook etc.).

Describe on this Journey Board how you started, your Small Steps Plan to promote your books, your Team, your struggle to define your very own Author Brand, your search for members of your Clan of Fierce Followers and Brand Ambassadors, your hunt for topics of value to your Target Reader Personas on your Author Blog, your ups and downs, your creative flashes, your trips to research places and events for your books, your work habits, your dreams and hopes, where you write (your desk, what you look at when you dream of scenes).

Add a *Pin It* button to your Author Blog and Facebook page. Add your book's name underneath your signature.

Invite Friends to your boards with that Pinterest tool.

10   *Pinterest and Your Next Book* –

Ask your Clan to pin pictures of places and events and people that you are considering using in your next book: it's a way to welcome them to help you write it, by fueling your imagination. Sign them up via your email sign up form, so that they can get prior copies of chapters when they are ready. You are giving your Clan bragging rights through engagement and early notice of your book's birthing. Invite them to share the struggle, and the triumph.

11   *Use Pinterest for Collaboration* –

Collaborate with your own Writers Club for a few shared Pinterest Boards (don't forget the pictures from your own past as part of the bios of the members of the Writers Club).

The shared board can be made accessible by all the Club members.

Now think of how to engage your Brand Ambassadors in a collaborative effort with your promotion plan, and/or your next book.

Watch the trends on Pinterest by clicking on *Popular* at the top of the site. Can you do some trend surfing by riding the wave of the moment while linking your promotional messages to it?

12   *Hyperlink text with Pin It –*
You use highlighted text in your blog posts hyperlinked back to the website the text refers to; you can do the same by highlighting text before you click the Pin It button – your highlighted text automatically populates your description.

13   *Author Blog Images –*
Your Author Blog images should be added to your Pinterest boards (with links back to your blog posts).

14   *Your Clan Board –*
Perhaps you could start a Clan of Followers board on Pinterest and ask your readers to pin photos of themselves on it along with a brief bio (but to take care about personal information because your Board is public)?

15   *Some Other Boards –*
One imaginative writer has a collection of Pinterest boards dealing with writing, including covers of books worth reading, pics of libraries, pics of bookshelves with books on them, author photos (consider Photoshopping them to add a new twist?), imaginary things, the art of writing, quotes by authors.

16   You & Pinterest & Contests:
How can you add contests, your book, and Pinterest together to make a Hook that takes people to your Author Blog and/or your Amazon Author Central page (where they can buy your eBooks)?

Brainstorm this with your Dream Team and do some Google searching for ideas; ask your Clan in your email messages, Pinterest boards and blog posts to find examples of interesting Pinterest contests. How about movie star pics for your characters?

17   Book Bloggers on Pinterest:

Google *book bloggers on pinterest* for a site with a listing of book bloggers on Pinterest. Follow some. Join it. Consider a collaborative project with other Indies to compile your own combined list of book bloggers and Indie writers on Pinterest.

1   **What is Twitter?**

Twitter is very confusing when you first join it, unless you understand what it does.

Think of Twitter as being <u>a separate cyberspace universe, a Twittersphere</u>, that exists somewhere out there. In that separate universe, there is a huge stream of cyberspace messages, called tweets, sent out every day by Twitter users – more than half a billion each day.

Nobody can read those tweets unless one of two things happens:

1. they have signed up via Twitter as a follower of the person sending out the tweet, or
2. they are followers of a third person, who reads a tweet and decides to send it out to his own followers, by repeating it (called *retweeting*).

So when you first start Twitter, you have no followers and are following no-one, so you cannot send tweets that will be read or read tweets that others have sent.

Your first order of business is:

a) <u>to follow people</u>, so that you can read their tweets or their retweets of other people's tweets, and
b) your second job is <u>to find people to follow you</u>, so that they can read your tweets.

2 **So how do you follow or find people to follow you?**

So who do you follow and how can you find people to follow you?

Twitter tries to help you when you sign up, by offering to find your existing contacts (on Gmail or Facebook) who might also have Twitter, and sending them a message that you are following them.

Twitter also tries to recommend people you might want to follow, to get your started.

And you can try to find people to follow and people to follow you by using your own email lists and Facebook and Author Blog posts to send out invitations to the people you know or who might read your Newsletter or Facebook or blog posts.

Another way to find people to follow (who might want to follow you in return), is to find lists of tweeters. You can create your own Lists, and you can read lists made up by other Twitter users (such as lists of writers, jugglers, knitters, joggers etc.).

3 **Why are you tweeting?**

That leaves you with another problem: Why are you tweeting?

Most users send out nonsense tweets (*I am eating a fig*).

But for you the answer is clear: you are trying to achieve your three main goals of your Small Steps Plan (email signup, joining your Clan, and converting to your Brand Ambassador). So stick to trying to achieve those goals when you tweet.

4   Empty tweets and tweets with luggage:

Another point to note is that there are **empty tweets** and **tweets with luggage**. Empty tweets are just the tweet itself (*I am eating a fig*).

A tweet with luggage is a powerful thing: it allows those who read the short tweet to go on to see or read a lot more, because it has a link to a separate video or website or blog post. That luggage is valuable, and is the reason why tweets with luggage are retweeted more often than empty tweets.

5   Now on with the details:

Twitter is a real-time network, open to everyone, where you can share your thoughts, or information, in a short message.

A tweet is a single update of 140 characters or less.

Your tweets appear in the *Twitter stream of your followers*, and of nobody else, unless one of your followers retweets you.

And just because your tweets appear in somebody's stream, this does **not** mean they will read it: most tweets die unread.

If you use someone's name in the *@mentions* feature (you add @theirname to your tweet) then they *might* read your tweet even though they are not following you (see below).

6   Your Twitter job:

Your job under your Small Steps Plan is:
1.   to increase the number of your followers, and
2.   to increase the reading rate of your tweets.

Other Twitter details:

Just to get a flavor of how Twitter works, here are a few general details:

7 *Twitter terms* –

Google *twitter help center twitter glossary* for a list of Twitter terms.

8 *Hashtags* –

Think of **hashtags** as the collie dogs in the pasture with the sheep. You use a hashtag (the # sign plus a word or phrase or topic) to begin and continue a conversation about that topic; a user who searches for that hashtag will find all the tweets that have that hashtag. So your hashtag is the collie dog of Twitterdom, sorting out all the sheep (tweets) in one place for you to read.

9 *More about followers and following* -

The Essence of Twitter = Followers, and perhaps Followers of Followers.

You follow someone to see their tweets; they follow you to see your tweets. The Twitter network connects people through this Follower link. And it goes further: if I retweet your tweet, then my followers will read your tweet; if they then retweet it, then their followers can see your tweet as well. Your tweet might never end!

You cannot stop someone following you, and you can follow anyone as well.

You click on the *@connect* button on the top left of your Twitter page to see who is Following you and who retweeted your tweets.

You can find out who to follow by clicking on the #Discover tab (you will also find stories, Find Friends, and Browse Categories there). Twitter gives you access to people all over the world.

10   *Manual on Twitter* -
Google *tweet right nicola morgan* for her detailed manual on Twitter (available as an eBook).

Or else for a free helping hand, Google *dummies.com understanding twitter basics* for a crash course in Twitter.

11   *Good and bad Tweeters* -
There are good Twitterers and bad Twitterers. The good ones share news, information, content of value to people. They are the ones who end up with a lot of followers. The bad ones share their personal drivel.

12   *Where to tweet from* -
You can tweet on your computer, your iPhone, via text-message: wherever you can access the Internet.

13   *How to reply to a tweet* -
Click the Reply button if you want to reply to a particular tweet. Or type @username and then your tweet, in the What's Happening? text box.

14   **Who reads Twitter?**
One recent study of US twitters showed that 55% were female and 45% male;

For more statistics on who uses Twitter (a 2010 study), Google *hubspot the ultimate list 100 twitter statistics*. Among these:

- only 5% have more than 100 followers;
- some 5% create 75% of all tweets;
- half have not tweeted in the past week (lazy Twitterers);
- Monday is the peak day for retweets;
- real life issues are most often tweeted on weekends;
- some 40% of tweets are 'babble', 38% chatty, 8% worth retweeting;
- around 30% of tweets are about the current status of users, while another 27% are private conversations; and
- tweets with links to news and blog articles total 10% of all tweets.

15   Who will read your Tweets?

All those who follow you, and the followers of those who retweet you, may, if they so wish, read your tweets.

Most will not, because there are close to half a billion tweets each day, and most are not read.

Those followers who find you interesting, might add you to a special list of people that they read on a regular basis.

Your job is to make people *want* to read your tweets. Start off with the assumption that very, very few will read your tweets.

Why do you as author need to Tweet?
16   Some reasons why:

Google *new york times why authors tweet* for an interesting take on this in 2012 by Anne Trubek. Salman

Rushdie said he liked Twitter because it allowed him to be playful. Another author writes in the voice of his dog.

You can learn by reading tweets from people who know what they are talking about; you can promote yourself but discreetly; you can network with people from all over the world.

TIP: Google *best authors on twitter* for lists of such authors. Follow a few to see how they handle Twitter. Can you do the same?

TIP: Google *why writers use twitter* for articles by or for authors on how best to use Twitter.

17   Twitter & Your Virality

Twitter might help your blog posts in your Author Blog go viral. Going viral is an elastic term, and it's best that you think of *virality* (the going viral of something on the social networks) as being a spectrum.

You are zero on that spectrum; the really successful people and products and events are in the upper 20 (from 80 to 100) of the spectrum.

Your chances of getting your virality up to that area are slim to zero; however, a more realistic target for you just starting out on your Indie author Journey, is to think of how to use your various social network channels to boost your virality from zero to say 1, then 5 and perhaps even as high as 10.

That's far more than it now is, and much, much higher than you would reach without your Small Steps Plan.

Going viral on Twitter means multiple retweets.

Rather than think about going viral on Twitter, your Small Steps Plan should aim at arriving at a set number of **quality** Twitter followers – remember John Lock and his initial goal of 100 Twitter followers.

18   How to use Twitter as an Author:

Meryl's Notes Blog had an article in 2009 headed *50+ Writer Uses for Twitter*, that you should glance at, for starters, and then Google *best writer uses for twitter* for more posts by others. Among her suggestions:

- Post story ideas and invite comments;
- Ask questions related to your story you are working on;
- Ask experts on a topic to help you;
- Join group chats for new ideas and insights (try #writechat);
- Issue story or Journey updates;
- Find guest bloggers;
- Post your promotion goals and report on your progress;
- Post links to free downloads.
- Above all, make sure your tweets fit your Author Brand.

TIP: Google *mashable 100+ of the best authors on twitter* and study a few in your own genre. What are they doing that you are not doing? Should you follow them? Send Direct Messages to them if you hit a bump in the road? And then Google *mashable authors* for a list of other good posts to dip into.

TIP: And Google *wow-womenonwriting.com* *time to twitter* for some good introductory information for authors on Twitter; then bookmark the wow site for later reference.

Building your Twitter content of your Small Steps Plan:

19   Remember your three major Promotion goals:

You use Twitter to achieve the *Joining* and *Conversion* parts of your 3 primary goals in your Small Steps Plan, which are:

Email - to obtain email addresses and consent to send further messages to those readers (see Task 11). This gives you the chance to send personalized messages to them on a frequent, carefully planned basis, as John Locke does.

Joining - you want to engage them enough to convert them into your Clan of Followers, and buy your books (see Task 4). You want them to *want* to read your social network messages, to follow you with enjoyment.

Conversion – you want to convert them into your Brand Ambassadors so that they proactively promote you and your books, including, as John Locke aims for, having them review his latest book(s).

Everything you do in your Small Steps Plan must have at least these three primary goals.

20   Your Editorial Content Plan:

Planning what to say on Twitter seems like an impossible mountain at first, but you are lucky: your ***Editorial Content Plan (ECP)*** will help you be methodical about it. Your tweets will fold into the themes and events you plan for various months and weeks, matching and reinforcing your posts in your Author.

21 Your Target Markets:

Step 1 in setting up your Twitter part of your overall Small Steps Plan (the roof of your Author Platform House), is to define your target markets before you start your Twitter promotions (see Task 3).

Think about your **Target Reader Persona**s each time you decide to tweet. Are you meeting their three main needs for using social networks (to be entertained; to nurture their friends and family; and to learn)?

22 Your Twitter Goals:

Consider which of these aims your various tweets are for:

- Are you trying to find story ideas?
- Or to promote your expertise in a way that fits your Author Brand?
- Or to do research?
- Or to drive traffic to your posts in your Author Blog?
- Or to engage your Target Readers?

Plan your Twitter conversations around your book's genre, themes, localities, scenes, characters, as well as your Personas.

And inject yourself into the mix: readers want to know who You are, what makes you tick, what makes you interesting, why they should Follow you.

Google *tips for using twitter: penny sansevieri* for some solid ideas on what you can offer as a writer to the world of Twitterdom.

Brainstorm Penny's ideas with your Team, and your Brand Ambassadors. Perhaps your Writers Club can cooperate on providing some of the value-added ideas?

Include a **tweet following strategy** as part of your Small Steps Plan. Find out who is following your major competitors, and if they are interesting, add them to your own Lists and follow them.

How can you use Twitter as an author? Here are some ways:

1. To find new Target Readers and persuade them to join your Clan;
2. To convert your Target Readers into your Brand Ambassadors by using your tweets and their tweets to engage them;
3. To talk to other writers about their writing and their promotion campaigns;
4. To invite your Target Readers and Clan to check out your Author Blog and your other promotion channels;
5. To alert your Target Readers and Clan to your planned events, promotional messages, contests and other matters.
6. How often should you tweet? Far less than you think. Twice a day could be the upper limit.

23   Prepare your Twitter Introduction and Biography:

You need a Profile on Twitter. Your profile might be a major influencer in people's decision whether to follow you. Is it clear who you are and why people should follow you?

Is it clear what your Twitter Followers will get if they follow you?

Think of your Personas when writing your Profile (but don't forget *Rebecca Random* and *Power Buyer Penny*).

Mention your book.

TIP: One of your tasks for your Small Steps Plan is to dip into the bios of other authors and other Twitters to see what they have in their Profiles; use a rating scale of 1 to 5 to keep track of the best ones (the 5's).

Google *can having a twitter bio get you 8 times as many followers dan zarrella* for a 2009 article on the importance of your Profile. Power followers (power users of Twitter) were twice as likely to follow you if you had a bio and a link (over 15 times for power followers than without a bio or links).

In another study Dan Zarrella found that users with the word *guru* or *expert* in their title had more followers than those without. If the user's Profile said she was a marketer or an entrepreneur, they tended to have more followers.

Google *meylah top 10 tips for writing a killer about page* for some solid hints (including: write in first person, using me, I; state your mission as a business or individual; let your You shine through).

Google *6 tips for using your twitter profile to get new followers* as well (using a custom background for your Twitter account; using a Twitter landing page and what to put on it).

24   How to start Tweeting:

If you get stuck with starting conversations on Twitter, Google *how to start a conversation on twitter* for some ideas of how to open up the conversation.

Dana Lynn Smith has some good suggestions for you in her 2011 article *Promote a Book with Twitter: Top Ten Strategies for Authors.*

Google *dummies.com twitter for dummies cheat sheet* for some nifty hints on what to do and not to do on Twitter. Read the one in the 8 series of articles about how to choose your Twitter name (click on the word Twitter in the heading, it takes you to a list of other articles).

Check out these ***hashtags for authors*** to give you a running start:

#amwriting
#author
#booktour
#bookreview
#fictionfriday
#selfpublishing
#writechat
#writing

TIP: Start your Twitter life with your first few tweets tweeting that you are starting your Journey as an Indie author; give an idea about what you will be doing to make that Journey successful; tweeting about your plans; make it interesting. Use some personal hashtags so that they can follow your tweets. I use #glennashton for my tweets.

TIP: Google *mashable The Beginner's Guide to Twitter* for a very good short introduction to Twitter.

Twitter Hashtags:

25   What are Hashtags?

Twitter users needed some way to group tweets that were on the same topic and so hashtags were invented: the # symbol to identify a topic or keyword in a tweet.

Hashtags are searched for using Twitter Search. Hashtags are also shortcuts to the folders where the tweets that contain a hashtag are stored: just click the hashtag and there you are!

Hashtags (#) create groupings of tweets around the word you applied it to. The hashtag becomes clickable and takes you to the folder to see all the other tweets with the same hashtag.

You can use the hashtag for an event, or a place, or a name, or anything you want to.

Where do hashtags go? Anywhere inside a tweet.

Hashtags are supposed to help readers of your tweets, not so let you show off. Don't use too many hashtags because they interrupt the flow of your tweets.

Make your hashtags meaningful because they lead to something dealing with the topic of your tweet.

26   Go to the Hashtags Gurus:

Bookmark ***hashtags.org*** and:

1. dip into the website for trending hashtags;
2. check the popular hashtags in different categories,
3. don't forget the hints on how to use hashtags;

4. click on How To in the right side bar under the heading Main Menu and see the wealth of articles about Twitter that you can read on the site;

5. read the sections under the heading Featured Resources in the right hand sidebar, especially Twitter for Newbies, How to Start a Hashtag, and Twitter Etiquette.

You can save any hashtag thread that your dip into regularly so that the saved hashtag list appears on your home page and you know what subjects you are monitoring and can access them easily.

Simply enter the hashtag into the Search box and then click *Save this search*.

Go to your Home page and click on the Searches tab (the magnifying glass) to see it on the dropdown menu.

You can also use Tweetdeck to save hashtags.

27   Who makes Hashtags?

Nobody controls hashtags; they live forever and are made by anyone.

And you should, too.

Give your Clan some folders to follow.

Do you write thrillers, like I do? Why not start a new hashtag for Indie authors, such as #indiethriller? And #indieromance? #indiemystery? #indiepromotion?

Tell your Target Readers about your new hashtags in your blog posts, tweets, on your Facebook etc.

Search hashtags.org to see if your new hashtag has already been used.

If not, define it on hastags.org.

Use your Headlines that Hook skills to compile catchy, short, powerful and memorable hashtags, and use your own hashtags on your Author Blog posts and in your tweets.

28   Where to find Hashtags:

Search for them on hashtags.org. Choose Tags on the top right, and then Directory from the drop down menu. You will see a jumble of alphabetical tags.

Or Google *twitter search* and then enter topics (e.g.: self publishing) to see what's being tweeted about on that topic, and check for hashtags to follow; or take a stab at any hashtags you think might fit what you are searching for.

29   Making your own Hashtags:

Brainstorm with your Team what kinds of hashtags you could use in order to lead people to your tweets, and polish your Author Brand.

Can you invent a few other hashtags that are related to you and your books, that are immediately powerful and easy to remember, and that your Clan can search for your tweets?

30   Hashtags for Authors:

Use the Twitter search to find topics you are interested in and then follow those hashtags. Like children's books? Check out #kidlitchat.

Want to see what writers are talking about?

Check #writer, #FollowFriday and #WriterWednesday. And #MentionMonday, #99centnetwork and #fridayreads.

Others are #MustRead, #goodread, #amreading, #scifichat, and #Yalit.

If you recommend someone to follow on these hashtags (Twitter communities), <u>make sure you have a good reason for doing this</u> and explain the reason, otherwise you will just clutter up the Twittersphere with more drivel. Your recommendations reflect on you and impact your Author Brand.

31   Hashtag recommendations for you to follow:

Google *Twitter hashtags authors* and *Twitter hashtags indie authors* for some to use.

Such as #IndiePub, #SelfPublishing, #Indiepubchat, #IndieAuthors, #bookmarketing, and #KindleChat.

Google *twitter search* and then bookmark the search page that appears; search the hashtags set out above to see who's saying what about them right now.

Going the extra mile with a carefully thought out reason why you recommend someone be followed on Follow Friday pays dividends: the person you are recommending sees that you have applied your mind to it rather than just dashed it off.

This is the kind of glue that cements relationships on Twitter.

32   Twitter Direct Messages:

A Direct Message is a message written to one specific person, not to the whole world. Direct Messages are a way to take tweets *out of* the worldwide Twittersphere, so that two people can talk to each other without the whole world listening in and joining in.

How do you send a Direct Message? Type D and then the username of the person you are sending your message to (d[username]), and then enter your message in the What's Happening? text box. You can also use your Messages Inbox in your profile to send Direct Messages to people.

You can only send a Direct Message (DM) to someone who is following you. So you get to decide who can send you Direct Messages when you decide to follow someone else, and they get to decide if you can send DMs to them when they decide to follow you.

Twitter Mentions:

33   What are Twitter Mentions?

If you include the @ sign followed directly by a username, this is a mention of that person.

All tweets with a mention are automatically sent to the person mentioned and park themselves in that person's list of Mentions. They remain unread until that person checks their Mentions.

If you Retweet someone, leave a space before you add the Mention; for example TW @username.

The person mentioned can Reply to that tweet.

If your tweet starts with @username, it is a Reply to another user and it appears on that other user's public stream and on yours. The person you replied to will see it, and so will her followers. And you will see it and your followers.

If @username appears <u>anywhere else</u> in the tweet, it is a Mention, not a Reply.

You can see who mentioned you by clicking on the @Connect tab at the top of your Twitter home page; the drop down menu includes a Mentions tab that shows all your mentions by others.

34   Who makes Twitter Mentions?
Anybody.

35   What to do if someone Mentions you
Check it out and thank them if you think it deserves thanks.

36   Twitter Etiquette and Rules:

Check hashtags.org for Twitter etiquette.

Vanessa Doctor in *Twitter Etiquette in 5 Ways* lays down 5 principles to guide you regarding etiquette:

- Cherish your relationships (than those who re-tweet or mention you, and engage in conversations);
- Learn how hashtags work (use them sparingly and with meaning);
- You are what you tweet (if you post drivel or embarrassing events or pics, remember that this stuff lives forever);
- Know you audience (and add value for them); and
- When in doubt, use your common sense.

Open up and engage with Twitters; you don't need an invitation. Engage in some small talk, thank people for retweeting you, compliment writers of good tweets or who link to good stuff you enjoyed.

<u>Give reasons why you are thanking them – be specific.</u>

<u>Check your @replies and RTs and pay attention to these people</u>: they are like those who comment on your posts on your Author Blog – more engaged, and a higher possibility for your 3 major goals (email, joining, conversion).

TIP: *You, Your Shotgun and Your Rifle* - Try two Twitter strategies when you start Tweeting – the shotgun and the rifle approach. With a shotgun strategy you aim at a wide audience, hoping to attract followers whom you can later focus on. With a rifle approach, you aim more carefully at your target markets – your Target Readers – with tighter messages.

And don't send personal information to anyone unless you know them well, and have a good reason to do so.

TIPS for Promoting using Twitter:

37   Using Twitter Chats:

Add as a t*ask* to your Small Steps Plan your participation in selected Twitter chats that will help you achieve your promotion goals.

Twitter chats help you to learn things, and also drive traffic to your Author Blog, and to get more Twitter followers.

Some valuable sites for you to check about Twitter chats:

- Google *socialmediaexplorer twitter chats* for an article on using Twitter chats as part of your social media strategy. Bookmark the *socialmediaexplorer* site and ask them to send you their report on the industry.
- Google *inkygirl writechat directory* for a list of Twitter chats for writers. And don't forget to Google *twitter chats for writers* for even more to consider. Here's a few for you to think about: #litchat, #poetry, #indiechat, #kidlitchat.
- And read *The Massive Guide on How to Get Involved in and Host Twitter Chats* by sociable-boost.com. Chats use a specific hashtag, and usually take place at a specific time. The chat host kicks things off and asks for comments. The host might pose a question or simply introduce the topic; you have to use the chat hashtag to join in.

Let your Clan know about your proposed Twitter Chats ahead of time, so that they can join in.

38   What does a Twitter Chat do for you as a writer?

Here are some benefits:

- It increases your visibility and so polishes your Author Brand;
- it engages your Clan if they take part;
- it can lead to finding interesting people to follow;

- it can help you learn things you never knew;
- it gives you a chance to send targeted messages to your Twitter Lists using retweets of comments made by others during your Twitter Chat.

TIP: *Twitter Chats* – consider posts on your *Author Blog* with lists of Twitter Chats of interest to your Target Readers Personas and other readers (and other lists for Indie writers and other segments you can think of). Jot down Twitter chats in your **My Bloggy Book** for later use in your blog posts.

For an interesting discussion of how to use Twitter Chats to change the one-way Twitter conversations into two-way macrologues, read Juliet Barbara's article in Forbes entitled *How Twitter Chats will Open Your Mind and Network* (Google the title). She writes about serendipitous connections that can arise in the liquid environment of a Twitter chat, and says she likes #Innochat and #Ideachat as well as #SocialMedia, and gives the link to a massive spreadsheet of chats.

TIP: *Twitter Chats & Your Writers Club* – having each one of your Writers Club members take turns to host a Twitter Chat on one of a series of chats on topics of interest to your mutual Target Readers, makes sense: spreads the workload, develops the Indie Community, and gives all the writers visibility. All members will then promote the chats. See if you can make it a regular weekly chat (set date and time with a catchy title so everyone knows when to tune in).

TIP: *Twitter Chats & Your Virtual Book Clubs* – set up (with your Writers Club?) biweekly Twitter Chats with all of your virtual book clubs, on set topics and chosen eBooks (free ones?).

39   **Making friends with Twitter:**

Keep the number small to start off, but remember what John Locke advocates (Task 3): build your following one person at a time. He writes that he has around 100 close Twitter friends who became email friends and now most are on his Guaranteed Buyer's List.

If you are asking people to be friends, introduce your-self, explain why you want to connect with them, and make sure they can see at a glance that there might be value in this for them.

It's hard work.

So pace yourself, set your goals and take your small steps while celebrating your small wins. Quality is better than quantity. Dip your toe into the stream and paddle carefully and with your goals firmly in mind.

You can have your email contacts (those you want) in-vited to join Twitter when you set up your Twitter account. Later on, you can invite them by clicking on the Who to Follow link and entering email addresses (commas and a space to separate them), then click Invite.

TIP: The more personal way is a personal email to each person, explaining what you are planning on Twitter and why you are inviting them to follow you, and why it could be a win-win.

40   Building promotional contacts with Twitter:

Twitter lets you engage with your readers and those who buy your books, on a less formal basis.

Let your *You* shine through, so they can see who you are, why your write, how your write and what you are trying to do. The Story of Your Journey.

TIP: See if Dana Lynn Smith has any suggestions you might like to adopt in her 2011 article *Promote a Book with Twitter: Top Ten Strategies for Authors.*

And remember what one author said he had learned: Twitter friends don't often buy books or give reviews but Twitter *email* friends do.

TIP: *Twitter EMAIL Friends* – One of your goals in your Small Steps Plan is to convert Twitter friends into Twitter Email Friends.

TIP: *Create your own Twibe* – Go to Twibe.com, search Writers and see if any existing Twitter Tribes suits you; if not, why not create one yourself, and invite your Writers Club and Brand Ambassadors to join it with you?

Check out *Twittgroups.com* as well.

41   Getting Help with Twitter:

Stuck in a rut? Use Twitter to cry for help.
Need help with a character? Try Twitter.

Want to know what a locality looks like for a scene in your next book or blog post? Ask via Twitter for links to what you want.

42   Polish your Platform & Author Brand with Twitter:

Always keep your focus on your Author Brand.

Be discreet – remember the 3 major needs of people who use social networks (entertainment, nurturing their friends, learning): if your tweet is not meeting at least one of those needs, why are you sending it out?

Here are the opinions of some writers on how to promote on Twitter:

- Mention special accomplishments, but then do virtually no self-promotion; let your friends to that for you and respond to their comments, adding a little bit as you do;
- Only promote yourself in passing;
- Make your tweets so interesting that people want to know more about you and click on your Profile; let your Profile do your talking.

43   Boost your Blog with Twitter – but carefully:

Just throwing up links to your blog posts is boring and ineffective.

Unless your blog post title has a Headline that Hooks, you should give people a reason why to read your blog post. Polish those tweets, make then enticing.

Make them irresistible. Your chances are good: most of the stuff tweeted is junk.

44   Teasers from your book on Twitter:

If you are about to launch a new book, use Twitter to tease your readers, over time, including excerpts, character descriptions, tweets by your characters.

45   Timing your Tweet is critical:

Tweet sparingly (many recommend a max of 2 a day, if that). Check what Dan Zarrella has to say about what day and what time of day to tweet about what topics. His blog is worth bookmarking.

46   Retweet! Retweet! Retweet!

Retweet or RT means to repeat someone else's tweet by sending it out as part of your own tweet. It is a way to make tweets go forth and multiply.

One assumption in one study by Dan Zarrella was that tweets posted during Eastern Standard Time business morning hours (9a.m. to 12 noon) in the USA ended up being retweeted more often. It seems getting them while they are fresh and just having their coffee works!

Dan Zarrella has also observed what he calls **ReTweet Cascades**: if people see retweets, they tend to retweet themselves, perhaps because retweeting is the Twitter social proof. The more retweets the more likely it is to be retweeted.

Ask for retweets, but use the whole word *Please Retweet* rather than RT – one study showed it resulted in more retweets.

TIP: A wise Retweet is an indirect Compliment to the original Tweeter!

For more hints on how to boost your retweeting rate, read Allyson Kapin's 2009 article on Dan Zarrella's study of retweeting, headed *The Art of Getting ReTweeted* – check reference on the right hand column. Among Dan's findings:

1. Dan studied 5 million tweets and 40 million re-tweets and compared them (when were they sent, which words and url shorteners were used most often etc.)
2. He thinks you should aim at 'contagious' tweets rather than at 'engaging' with others on Twitter (he thinks engagement on Twitter is not 'actionable advice');
3. Use bit.ly or others to shorten URLs because they are three times more retweetable than longer urls or tinyurl;
4. Asking *Please Retweet* this is very retweetable (calls to action work!).
5. Mondays and Fridays appear to be the days there are more retweets, according to Frogloop.
6. Leave 25 characters of free space in your tweets so that others can add the RT and @username to retweet them.
7. What seems to be retweeted often? Lists do; re-tweeting blog posts is popular.

One author found that a good dollop of emotion result-ed in a jump in retweets. Make them angry or make them laugh, and they will retweet. So, don't just paddle in that Twitter stream: splash about, arouse emotions, fire them up, make them weep, forgeddabout placidity.

TIP: *How to streamline your Retweeting* - Google *my 6 step plan to give thanks to my followers* for an article on *twitip* about how one tweeter nurtures followers.

One method is to make a list of all those who retweet his tweets (called **My Top Retweets**) as this makes it easier for him to follow their tweets (when you go to a List only the tweets of those users on the List show in your stream).

And this gives him a chance to focus on returning the favor by retweeting some of their tweets in the reduced stream he is seeing.

TIPS on using Twitter well:

47 *Join Twitter Chats:*

Google *inkygirl twitter chats for writers* for ideas about Twitter chats you might wish to explore; check out Weekly Chats at a Glance.

48 *Start Twitter Contests:*

Check the Twitter Help Centre for their Guidelines for using Contests on Twitter, and think about starting one yourself (perhaps a monthly one?).

49 *How are you doing?*

You can measure a Twitter accounts influence using **Tweetgrader**. You enter the Twitter user name and it gives you a summary of the ranking of the account and the grade.

50 ***Tools to Beef up your Twitter Presence:***

Google *The Top 100 Twitter Tools of 2012 (Categorized)* for a March 2012 listing in various categories. Browse through them and select a few to use on a regular basis, and let your Target Readers know via all your social network channels (Author Blog, virtual Newsletter, Twitter etc.). Ask your Clan to use some of the same, and each quarter ask for feedback so that you can compile a Clan Comparison Report showing the averages.

TIPS for building Followers:

51   Follow carefully – do your homework first:

Be ruthless in deciding who to follow. Unless they can help you achieve the goals of your Small Steps Plan, don't just follow them. Cap the number of followers so that you have a more manageable stream to dip into.

Quality trumps quantity, for purposes of your Small Steps Plan.

Only follow those who produce quality tweets.

Let me repeat that.

Only follow those who produce quality tweets.

Why?

Because a big source of your attraction as a Tweeter will be the quality of your own retweets. So start with quality tweets from the people you follow, and the quality of your own retweets will be higher.

Remember, most tweets are junk.

And your Author Brand is not junk; it is you, your essence as a writer. That is something to treasure, and one way to do that is to guard against diminishing it.

Do your homework on those you might follow: read their tweets carefully and see if they meet your high standards. Read their bio carefully. Then check out who they follow or retweet and see if you would like to follow them.

If you like some bloggers, check if they tweet, and consider following them and retweeting their good posts and tweets.

Check the **Twitter Lists** on Twitter for potential people to follow. You can also use the **Tweetdeck Directory** to find lists (see below).

Bookmark *wefollow.com* and dip into the site using its search box to find prominent people in the category you entered, to check out for following. Try writers and see their rankings.

You can also check *ListAtlas* for lists of writers etc.

And post a few Tweets before your start following anyone, so that those you follow who check on you have something from your pen to judge you by when they decide whether to follow you in return.

52 Nurture your own followers:

Just as you should concentrate on the quality of those you follow, so too should you provide quality to those who follow you. It works both ways for people to maintain interest and engage in conversations.

You will nurture your followers successfully ONLY if you meet one or more of their three needs from social networks (entertainment, nurturing their own friends, and learning). You have to add value, on a consistent basis.

They must read your tweets and have a reason for taking time out to follow you regularly.

Think of your Target Readers Personas: think of what you would say if you were having a conversation with them, right now, in this very room. What would their 3 major needs be? What could you say to them that would meet those needs?

Google *dummies.com tips for engaging your twitter followers* for some solid pieces of advice on this topic. Note the advice that you should:

- share first before others with share your content;
- deal with the top 10 you are following and the top 10 that are following you, and focus on sharing their valuable content as much as you can and when you can;
- Direct Message those Top 10 to make contact with them;
- ask how you can help your followers and then deliver what is asked for;
- use **Klout** to find out the scores of your followers to decide which ones to focus on.

While you are there, check if you have any Klout.

53   General points on finding Followers:

1   *Ask for them* –

Ask for followers in a tweet and has your Twitter URL, that is: www.Twitter.com/yourusername.

Have the tweet link to a post on your Author Blog that describes your quest for quality followers, defines what kinds of followers you are looking for, and sets out very clearly what the quid pro quo is (what value do they get if they follow you?).

2   *TwitterPacks –*

Check whether you can use this site to locate people to follow (Klout them first ...). Google *david fleet how to use twitter pack – and twitter – successfully* for hints in 2008 on how to use this site.

3   Follow those who follow you:

But do your homework first: are they worth following? Will it help you towards achieving your promotion goals to follow them?

4   Follow that Blogger:

If you find very interesting blogs that fit with your goals in your Small Steps Plan, click on the Follow on Twitter button in those blogs.

5   Ask people who you should follow:

Consult your Dream Team, and your Target Readers, with links to your blog post on what type of people you want to follow and have as followers.

6   The Limit on the Number of Followers:

It's 2,000 maximum. Period. You cannot follow more people than that. When you hit 1,500, start unfollowing people who are not active, who are not better than others you can find to follow.

7   Run Debates on Twitter & your Author Blog about topics in your book:

Pose the moral or political or economic themes in your book as topics for a debate; create appropriate hashtags so that the debaters can tune in to the debate by going to the debate hashtag; invite your Target Readers to choose one side of the debate (for or against); invite other Target Readers to become your Debate Panel to decide which side one (need 5 to 10 criteria); organize a vote using one of the polling apps; award prizes to the entries judged best; and launch a series of debates.

You could pit supporters of some of your **Writers Club** members (the for group) against supporters of other members (the against group), with the supporters of the third group being the Debate Panel.

You could restrict the speakers in the debate to purely tweets (short, snappy answers), or allow links to one-paragraph posts in their blogs to explain their views (with a work maximum to stop endless diatribes), or to comments made on your Author Blog debate post, which set out their speeches (honor-bound limit on size of comments, perhaps).

Want to reward your **Clan**? Only Clan members (or **Brand Ambassadors**) can be judges on the Debate Panel.

Ask Clan members to suggest future debate topics, flowing from your book (scenes, questions raised, behavior of characters); let your **Target Readers** choose the order of the debates via polls.

Brainstorm with your **Team** how else to combine Twitter and your Author Blog in debates / discussions around your book.

TIPS for using Follower Lists effectively:

54   *What are Twitter Lists?*

Google *twitter how to use twitter lists* for the official rules governing Lists. Read them carefully.

Twitter says this about its Lists:

"A list is a curated group of Twitter users. You can create your own lists or subscribe to lists created by others. Viewing a list timeline will show you a stream of Tweets from only the users on that list."

The Lists feature lets you organize people you follow into your groups, or Lists. You can use Lists to organize your tweeting, and build followings around certain topics or events. You can add people you are not following into your Lists.

55 *Why make Lists?*

You can group the people you follow, and then just read the tweet stream for those on each List so as to follow the conversations better. You can then reply to tweets made by those on the List you are getting in your stream of tweets, to strike up or continue a conversation.

<u>Twitter Lists are designed only to carve out some tweets (those from people on your own Lists) from the vast ocean of Twitter tweets</u>, so that you can read those tweets by those people only and not be bombarded by tweets by all your followers.

Google *mashable twitter lists* for a set of Twitter lists; bookmark it.

Because Twitter does <u>not</u> allow you to send tweets only to those on your Lists (all your tweets go out to all your followers, not just to those followers you placed on your own List), and because you have to send Direct Messages to individuals, one at a time, and cannot use Direct Messages to send a tweet to those on your List, your Lists have limited value as a tool to start conversations with a limited number of people using Twitter.

But if you can persuade the people on your Twitter Lists to became email subscribers, you could start one on one or one on a group of conversations, outside Twitter.

Set up your very own *Quality Twitter Lists* –

As a task in your Small Steps Plan, go through your collection of Lists and select a dozen or so each month for quality-tweeting in the next month.

Name this List using the Month, Year and the word Quality: eg: March13Quality.

Then read the bios of all those on the monthly test list and decide what special quality treatment you can provide to them.

Because Lists are used for reading Tweets only, you cannot send a Tweet to members of a List for only those members to see. So your List only serves to show you a stream of tweets from those on your list.

You have to ask them individually to Follow you and if they do, to then send a Direct Message to them and ask if they would like to receive your Newsletter.

Experiment and see how many on your quality lists agree to join your email subscriber lists.

Use the ideas that work for future targeting.

56   *Your Keyword Lists –*

Put your book Keywords into the Twitter search box to find conversations about those keywords and check out the users:

- add them to your Keyword Lists (your titles for these lists should be Keyword List [the keyword]; eg: Keyword List [technothriller].
- Follow them and read their tweets;
- retweet their content;
- then Direct Message them with a blog post link that talks about what the significance of your Keyword is to you and asks them if they would like to engage in a Twitter conversation via DM and then later on,
- convert them to email subscribers.

TIP: Google *Twitter lists: a power tool for authors by freya* for a post on how using Lists can make your life as a Tweeter much, much simpler, and maximize your engagement possibilities with your followers.

57   *Your Private Lists –*
Public lists are the default choice, but you can create your own private lists for various purposes.

You could include your most important followers in such a list, for use with retweeting, or followfridays nominations etc.

Or your Writers Club members, or your Brand Ambassadors. Makes it easier to DM them, or follow their tweets and retweet etc.

Google *how to use twitter lists like a pro* for some hints, and then google *Twitter Enhances Lists: 4 Ways To Take Advantage* for more hints on private lists.

58   *Create your Rotating Followers Lists for special attention:*

This helps you nurture them more extensively, by breaking them out into groups (one per List), and then messaging them (retweets, replies, direct messages, mentions) without missing some.

Rotate your Lists for attention every now and then.

Google *ilovefreesoftware 5 free twitter alert services* and check out the free services that allow you to input keywords or topics and get emails alerting you to when they appear on Twitter. Check out especially **Twilert** and **TweetBeep** and **TweetAlarm**. Use the alerts to alert your followers on your various Lists about themes or discussions on their topics of interest. Add your name to the list so that you know when someone tweets about you.

59   *Have a Twitter Time each day:*

Discipline yourself with a Twitter time for each day, and put a limit on how much time you spend on Twitter or you will go down the mouse hole and get lost, lost, lost!

60   *Use Twitter Search:*

A search engine on Twitter. You can search keywords, hashtags, topics, people (to find their posts or posts about them), and you can filter the results to show only those that contain links or include retweets.

Google twitter search and bookmark the site in your search engine and other spots.

Use it to find tweets on topics relating to your Small Steps Plan messages; then retweet the good tweets, and follow the valuable tweeters.

Link to your Author Blog post on the topic (your targets are partly pre-selected because they tweeted about the topic).

TIP: *Stockpile your Twitter ammunition* - Make a list of good things about your subject matter, recent events etc. – save it and update it to provide fodder for focused, subject matter driven tweets, such as your **Weekly Tweets** planned for in your **Editorial Content Plan (ECP)**.

If you want to tweet about a location in your book, you can search for tweets near that location, using the keywords *near:*[location, e.g.: Seattle] or *within:*[25mi for 25 miles] as part of your search.

61   **Research your Twitter Competition**:

How to research them, and their Tweet Clouds:
Google *mashable 100+ of the best authors on twitter* and study a few in your own genre.

What are they doing that you are not doing? Should you follow them? Send Direct Messages to them if you hit a bump in the road?

What are you looking for?
- What they say.
- How they say it.
- What their links say and how the links say it.
- How they retweet.
- Who they retweet.
- How they promote.
- What their Author Brand is and whether their tweets fit it.
- What they have on their websites or blogs.

- What contests they use.
- Anything that makes you a better writer, tweet-er, blogger and promoter.

Add your name to any directories of authors and self published authors on Twitter that you find.

TIP: *You, Your Competition, and their Tweet Clouds* - Plug their Twitter username into Twitter Grader and check their Twitter profile, grade, website, and – very important! – their *Tweet Cloud* (Google Tweet Cloud and then book-mark it – use it every 3 months to discuss with your Team about your Twitter activities and whether they fit your Personas). If your major competitors are tweeting about topics or keywords as shown in their Tweet Clouds (words most often found in their tweets), and you are not, should you join those Tweet Clouds?

TIP: *Join the Tweet Clouds* of your major competitor authors and book promoters.

Compare the Tweet Clouds of various authors on Twitter (especially those with high ranks). What is common in their Tweet Clouds? Are you in those Clouds? If not, why not? Their Tweet Clouds are diamonds in the rough: you should get a pretty good idea what they are tweeting about from them.

What are they doing wrong with Twitter? How do you rate your Tweets against their Tweets? What are they doing when Tweeting that you are not doing? Who are they Following? Who is Following them? What do their Tweets tell you about their promotion methods?

62   Tweetdeck:

I've joined Tweetdeck and found it very useful; you should check it out and consider using it as well. It's free.

It lets you manage Twitter and Facebook accounts, and is now owned by Twitter.

You can arrange your feeds, focus on what matters to you, schedule your tweets and stay up to date with notification alerts for new tweets. You end up with three columns: AllFriends (tweets by those you follow: Mentions (when your name is used in a tweet); and Direct Messages (from your followers to you).

Play with Tweetdeck until you know how it works; schedule a few tweets and see how easy it is.

You can use your scheduled tweets for:

- spreading out messages if one tweet is too short;
- sending out parts of a tutorial you are publishing, or chapters of your book;
- tweeting a daily or weekly quote from your book or the books of your Writers Club or quotes sent to you by your Clan;
- tweets linked to future events or dates or seasons as per your **Editorial Contents Plan** (ECP);
- experimenting with different styles of tweet headlines and tweet publishing times (days of the week and/or time of day) to see what results in the most reaction;
- sending out snippets of information about your Clan members, based on their agreed submissions of info to you via your email subscription

list, with them spaced out so that you have a steady stream of Target Reader engagement messages going out to the streams of your Followers.

63   **Explore Twitter Tools:**

Once you are comfortable with Twitter, do some Google searches for the latest Twitter tools or widgets and then dig into them to see if any fit your needs. Experiment with those that might.

Google *mashable list of 140+ twitter tools* for some ideas!

TIP: *You, Your Clan & GroupTweet* - Consider using GroupTweet for tweets to one Twitter account from your Clan members, and/or your Brand Ambassadors, and/or your virtual Book Club, and/or your Writers Club. Make this a task in your Small Steps Plan.

GroupTweet lets from 2 to 100,000 people send tweets to one Twitter account. You can moderate the messages and arrange the scheduling for the tweets. You can have the tweeters identified or their names hidden.

Brainstorm with your Team and Brand Ambassadors how best to use GroupTweet in your Twitter Plan. You could select themes and have the Clan grouptweet about it. Use GroupTweet to hold your Twitter Debates (see above) with only Clan members being able to tweet?

Google *twitter tools* for other suggestions. Google each tool to make sure you read about them before you experiment with them.

TIP: *FollowerWonk & Your Competition* – Try a dynamite Twitter tool (free) that is named *followerwonk* to learn about those any Twitter user follows.

Once you've signed up, you can plug in the Twitter username of anybody, and it will analyse those tweeters that that user follows.

So plug in your competing authors' usernames and see who *they* are following: you see a map showing where in the world they are; an analysis of their gender and age; languages used; percentage of tweets with URLs; retweets as a percent of timelines; most active hours they tweet; bio word cloud of the users. Neat stuff!

Google *New Buddy Media Data: Strategies for Effective Tweeting: A Statistical Review* for a fascinating 2012 study (with diagrams) of what to tweet and when to tweet it.

Google *lists of self-published twitter authors* for a list; study how some of them are using Twitter.

1   Why use email to promote your book?

Email gives you a direct link with those who agree to receive regular emails from you. You <u>need</u> direct links (via shared emails, or direct messages on Twitter, or direct messages on Facebook) <u>in order to build a personal relationship</u>. And personal, one-on-one relationships are the way to build your Clan and convert them into Brand Ambassadors.

2   Preparing your Email Plan:

Your Email part of your Small Steps Plan is for the long-term, so concentrate on Small Steps in starting if off, and Small Wins. Rome was not built in a day.

Your ***Editorial Content Plan*** must include your *schedule* for your email program, and you must give some thought to the *content* of your various messages via emails.

You need to get people <u>to agree to sign up as subscribers</u> for more emails and any newsletters you wish to email them. Do not spam people; it is also illegal in many places.

3   Hint: Hook them or Lose them – Why should they read your email?

You've got between 3 and 5 seconds to hook their interest or they will flee with a click.

How can you tell them what benefits they will get from reading your email *now*?

Flag it with a table of contents or *In This Issue* near the beginning of your email.

Or: *Today you will read about ....*

Or: *You might have a friend who would like to know ....*

Or: *Stay on top with these ....*

TIP: ***Always, always, always Ask!*** – Many people fail to clinch sales because they just don't actually ask people to buy their products. You want anybody who reads your blog posts or your tweets or sees your videos or reads your comments in forums, to want to agree to become a member of your Clan and your Brand Ambassador. *They won't do this unless you ask them to do it* – clearly, repeatedly, charmingly. So ask. Make it a polite ask, but ask.

Your email plan is one way to ask, ask and ask.

4   Goals of your Email Plan:

Your 3 primary goals apply to your Email part of your Small Steps Plan [To build up solid, friendly relationships with my Target Readers, so as to convert them into members of my Clan, and then to turn some of them into my Brand Ambassadors.]

You will also have specific goals for your email campaigns. Some suggestions are set out below (written in first person so that you can simply add them to your own Small Steps Plan if you want to).

Bounce your plan for each email campaign off your Team, to make sure the goals are clear, the target readers are clear, and the contents will enable you to achieve your goals for that campaign.

VERY IMPORTANT TIP: Google *Got Content? Great, Now Let's Grow Your Email ROI AWeber* for some solid hints on how to work out your strategy for using your email as part of your Email Plan. Get the report. It covers setting goals for your email campaign; setting clear expectations for subscribers so as to increase sign ups; segmenting lists; automating your email campaigns; and optimizing and testing regularly.

ANOTHER VERY IMPORTANT TIP: Bookmark the AWeber site – it is almost like a college course in what emailing is, how to go about it, and how to make it work for you. Read as many of their articles as you need to, so as to become very comfortable with emailing.

5   Some Goals for your Email plan:

After setting out some goals for your Small Steps Plan, we will discuss specific parts of emailing and provide hints. Here are 20 possible goals for you to brainstorm with your Team:

6   Your Bigger Goals:

- **To create an email contact strategy –**
To create a new, ongoing email contact strategy in order to obtain as many subscribers for my email messages (including my Newsletter(s)) as possible in the next 12 months.

- **Engagement through reward –**
To provide good reasons for my target readers to become engaged with me, so that they purchase my book(s), become members of my Clan and Brand Ambassadors.

- **Subscriber list growth –**

To grow and maintain my email subscriber list, starting at zero, to [set a figure] signed up subscribers within 12 months. (Note: re-read John Locke's first goals in Task 3 above).

B: Your Smaller Goals:

Now break each of these bigger goals down into smaller steps. Here are 17 examples for you to consider:

7 Opt in Form –

To develop, after discussion with my Team, a multi-layer Opt In Form for use in obtaining sign ups by subscribers to my emails, by [insert due date].

8 Subscriber list kick start –

To kick start my email subscriber list, I will ask selected persons whose email addresses I already have, to sign up for my email program using the Opt In Form.

9 Subscriber list growth: Opt-In Form –

To add the Opt In Form to every social network channel I have (Facebook, Twitter, Author Blog, others?), by [insert due date].

10 Content value: Contagious –

To better engage my Target Readers, I will discuss with my Team the nature of "contagious" content for my email messages, based on my Target Reader Personas, by [insert due date].

11   Content value through questions –

To better engage my Target Readers, I will post 4 articles (1 every 3 months) on my Author Blog discussing what kinds of message content might appeal to my Target Reader Personas, and inviting responses from readers on what kind of content they think might add value to such Personas, and/or to themselves.

12   Frequency –

To better engage my Target Readers, I will prepare 12 articles of very high value content for emailing to my subscribers at the rate of one per month for the next 12 months.

13   Persona Research –

To better engage my Target Readers, I will prepare 4 quizzes (1 every 3 months) designed to obtain demographic and other information from my Target Readers, that will allow me to segment them into groups and thus allow more tailor made value-added messages to the segments. Responders to each quiz will be sent [state the type of rewards]

14   Automation of email delivery –

To set up and use a suitable email services company to allow me to send emails to my target reader segments, with suitable content and at times I choose, by [insert due date].

15   Learning curve –

To learn all the features of my email service provider by [insert due date], and to ensure that my Team knows the features and understands how they can help achieve my goals in my Email Plan by [insert due date].

16 Engagement through reward: PDF package –

To better engage my Target Readers, I will prepare 4 packages of high quality, value-added PDF documents, 1 every 3 months, for use as rewards for those who subscribe to receive my emails, and those who provide additional information to me so as to allow me to provide better services to them.

17 Monitoring: Tests –

To monitor the success rate of my email messages (as measured by click rates and click through rates) and to discuss at least once a quarter with my Team methods to improve these rates.

18 Engagement through reward: Webinar –

To prepare one Webinar as a reward for new email subscribers and existing subscribers, by [insert due date].

19 Research: Writers Club –

I will discuss with my Writers' Club the methods they use, or know other authors use, to set up and maintain a high quality email subscription program, by [insert due date].

20 Research: Forum Threads –

Once every 3 months, I will research the threads of the following Forums [insert names of forums] and through

Google for discussions of the use by authors of email contact programs, and advise my Team of the findings.

21   Monitoring: Split-Level Tests of From & Subject Lines, & Content –

I will use at least one split-level test for my emails to test the benefits of different content and headings, by [insert due date].

22   My Newsletter –

I will set up a regular digital Newsletter, to be delivered every [week][month] to my subscriber list, by [insert due date of startup of Newsletter], including allowing potential subscribers to access one web-based example of the Newsletter so that they understand exactly what they can expect to receive.

23   Research: Other Newsletters –

Once every 6 months, I will research digital Newsletters published by authors and other people, to see what hints I could get regarding quality, content, use of images, feedback requests, rewards for signups, engagement features, etc., starting on [insert date of start of research].

That will do to kick start your Email Plan.

Google *The Ultimate Email Glossary 178 common terms defined* and then bookmark it for future reference should you need to brush up on any email jargon.

24 Four Technical Terms you need to know right now:

Four technical terms you need to know at this stage follow:

*What is an **open rate** of an email? -*

It is the number of people who actually open your email.

*What is a **click rate** in an email? –*

It is the number of people who click on links in your email

*What are **Split Test**s? –*

A method to test two alternative subject line texts or message contents by splitting your list of subscribers into two segments and sending one email to the first list and the second to the second list, to see if response rates of subscribers are different.

*What is an **Autoresponder** –*

This is a computer program that automatically answers emails sent to it. You use it for marketing, as it provides immediate information subscribers when they sign-up and then follows-up with them at preset time intervals. So they are good for managing your messages to new subscribers on a regular, planned basis.

25 John Locke's use of email to promote his books:

John Locke - who wrote eBooks that sold more than a million copies - writes that his system requires personal responses to ALL emails you receive.

Personal responses.

He insists on the personal touch: whether the readers reach you via comments on your Author Blog or via Twitter or any other way.

He sends several hundred emails each day, aimed at a quick launch of his latest book. The recipients buy the book, and next day another email goes out to several hundred more on his email subscriber lists, driving sales even higher, creating an Amazon Rush; and he moves his books up the Amazon charts.

Locke is very clear: he built his reading audience one email at a time. He has a contact button on his website; those who like what they see, or read his post on a guest blog, contact him. And then, he says, "we're one step away from an email friendship".

TIPS on promoting your books using email:

Quality over Quantity:
Your emails MUST add value to your readers.
Let's repeat that.
Your emails MUST add value to your readers.
Value is in the eyes of the beholder, not necessarily yours.

A good email is a personal one. Think of your Target Reader Personas: make your messages to them personal.

Your Email Plan must provide for a consistent, target-ed, long term use of emails to achieve your Plan.

26   **Nurture your Feeders:**

Ask your email subscribers to send you ideas or tips or information meeting the 3 main needs of social network users ((entertainment; nurturing their friends; or learning). Thank them if they do.

Don't forget to ask them to spread the word to their friends. And when the post appears, send them another personal email thanking them again, with a link to the post.

TIP: *Success review* – Review with your Team every so often the open rates, click rates, calls to action and other success metrics of your emails, so as to sharpen your aim with future ones.

To personalize your welcome email to those subscribers who signed up to be on your email list, you might want to add a few words about your history as a writer, and your journey so far. Tweak their interest.

To encourage engagement, your later email messages could include carefully built polls and quizzes, or requests for reviews, and encouragement for participation in social network threads you are participating in or have started in a Forum.

You need good contact management services from your email service provider, allowing you to manage your subscriber lists (including unsubscribing), sign-up forms, autoresponders (a computer program that automatically answers emails sent to it), split-testing, and segmentation of your subscriber list.

Your new subscribers are very engaged at the moment they sign up; this is the time to provide them with information about you and your books. <u>Your autoresponder will allow you to plan for and deliver a sequence of emails automatically</u>. There should be a welcome email followed by others. You can schedule downloads for them, or information about your books. The follow-up messages should be personalized with your subscribers names and other information.

27   Your Signup Form:

This is a powerful weapon in your Email strategy. It MUST work if people are going to sign up to receive your regular emails and your digital Newsletter. See below for more on this feature.

TIP: Visit this site for articles on how to build your email list for your EMAIL Plan:

http://www.blogworld.com/2011/07/07/15-brilliant-bloggers-talk-about-list-building/

Your signup form should respond with two messages from you: the first welcomes the new subscriber, and the second has answers to the most popular questions about your site. These will be delivered automatically to sub-scribers when they sign up to your list.

Where do you find a signup form?

Wufoo has a free form maker that integrates with the free email service provider, MailChimp, to allow you to make your own sign up forms.

You can also make your own form with *Google Docs*. Go to the *bloggertipsandtricks* blog for an example of the form he built.

AWeber, one of the best email service providers, has oodles of possibilities when it comes to your signup form, dealt with in detail below.

28   Your Opt-In Thank-You & Guinea Pigs -

Perhaps you could get a running start at forming a Subscriber *Quality Test Guinea Pigs* Group by asking them to indicate if they would like to get emails from you that involve a small group of subscribers acting as guinea pigs to test future email messages (things like Headline Hooks, message content, call to action, layout, images) for you. Explain – through a link to a blog post or a downloadable PDF with clickable hyperlinks – what kind of responses these Quality Test Guinea Pigs would be expected to give, and why you wanted such tests.

29   Subscriber Expectations -

Making sure that your potential subscribers know **exactly** what to expect from your emails and Newsletters, including giving them the ability to actually read an example of your Newsletter before they sign up.

Google *5 steps to stronger email relationships AWeber* for access to a PDF study entitled that.

30   The 4 Questions -

Your opt in page should answer these 4 questions (what, when, why, and privacy):

What type of content will you get once you sign up? A link to a copy of the Newsletter answers this clearly.

When will you get the email messages? Let the subscriber choose from a menu how often.

Why should I sign up? Explain the benefits, from the subscribers point of view (what will the newsletter do for them? Solve what problems? Help them meet what challenges? Others?).

Privacy – Be clear what you will and won't do with their email address.

31   What to look for in an email service provider:

What you are looking for in an email service are templates (to help you design your emails), affordable pricing (ranging from free to very expensive), satisfactory delivery of your emails, and monitoring systems to track the results of the emails you send out.

Can the email service allow you to track the activities of those who click on the links in your emails, and analyze the results in a way that makes your future emails to them more focused and more effective? You need to know what is happening to your emails if you want to use this channel properly.

The list below gives you the most important items to consider when deciding on whose program to use (whether it be a free one – dealt with below – or a paid service, such as AWeber).

32   Factors your email service should provide you include:

Ease of use - You want to spend your time composing your messages with your Team rather than fiddling with a hard to understand and unclear email service.

Imports – Can you easily transfer (called import) your existing email lists into your new email service?

Segmenting of your target readers – You want to easily sort out the various groups of readers so that you can fashion detailed, targeted messages to each reader segment.

Good templates – You should not reinvent the wheel; your service should have good, easy to use templates for many tasks you will be carrying out.

Opt-in Form – Your service should have an easy to use opt-in form to let readers sign up to receive your email messages. If it is one you can edit to personalize it for your own uses, all the better.

Unsubscribe form – You need one; if you can edit it (see below for hints), good.

Links to social media – Can you easily link your Facebook, Twitter, Author Blog, YouTube and other social media to your emails?

Ability to experiment – Does the service allow you to test various parts of your email messages to find out what works the best? You are aiming at continuous improvement in your marketing messaging.

Drip-marketing – Can you plan drip-marketing campaigns, sending tailor made messages to different market segments over time? This will be another Task in your Email Plan.

Autoresponder – This is a computer program that automatically answers emails sent to it. You use it for marketing, as it provides immediate information subscribers when they sign-up and then follows-up with them at preset time intervals. So they are good for managing your messages to new subscribers on a regular, planned basis.

CAN-SPAM Act:

The CAN-SPAM Act is a U.S. law that requires commercial emails to offer an unsubscribe option and to contain the sender's valid physical postal address.

Google *Making Sure that Your E-Mail Marketing Complies with Spam Laws* and John Arnold for a good article explaining the CAN-SPAM Act of the USA.

33   Features of the AWeber email services program:

I recommend that you seriously consider the paid AWeber service if you are going to write more than one book, and will be setting up a credible Promotion Plan to market them.

AWeber was founded in 1998, and is a popular email marketing program.

Google *aweber* to go to their site and examine the information they provide, especially their Knowledge Base and Webinars.

TIP: *Aweber as Your Teacher* - Add as a Task to your Promotion Plan your reading of the *AWeber Knowledge Base* and *Webinars*.

Also, subscribe to the AWeber blog:
http://www.aweber.com/blog/

AWeber RSS to Email –

Allows you easily to turn your Author Blog posts into an email newsletter.

AWeber Costs –

Up to 500 subscribers and unlimited emails costs less than US$20 per month with AWeber, with increases for more subscribers. *MailChimp* is free for up to 2,000 subscribers, but its services do not allow use of most of the popular affiliate products.

AWeber Training –

AWeber has a good stable of ***Email 101*** lessons for you to learn all about using email to promote your book, including its Knowledge Base articles, Webinar series, and many Videos. Use these to learn even if you choose another email service.

AWeber Types of Messages –

AWeber allows you to choose one of 3 types of messages to send to your email subscribers: Follow up, Broadcast and Blog Broadcast Messages.

Follow up Messages go out automatically after people subscribe to your emails, and you stipulate the intervals (in days) before the next one goes out.

Broadcast Messages are sent at specific dates and times you chose; you can send Broadcast Messages to your segments of your subscriber lists, allowing you to tailor make your pitches to each segment. You use them for time sensitive messages, or seasonal ones, or for regular weekly or monthly Newsletters. You might use Broadcast Messages to new subscribers, in between the scheduled Follow up Messages.

Blog Broadcast Messages are created automatically whenever you make a new post on your Author Blog.

34   Some free email service providers you could check:

Among the email service providers you could check out are Constant Contact, MailChimp, Infusionsoft, JangoMail, VerticalResponse, iContact and, of course, AWeber (costs US$19 per month or $194 per year as of February 2013, for up to 500 subscribers).

List Wire is a **free** email service, including an autoresponder service. However, your subscribers get one email offer for products from Listwire when they opt-in to receiving your emails, and you will receive emails offering you products in return for using Listwire.

MailChimp is **free** for up to 2,000 subscribers, but its services do not allow use of most of the popular affiliate products; it is worth serious consideration. Visit their site and Google *mailchimp* for more information.

Check out the following email service providers to see what each one offers, and at what cost: Aweber, Mail-Chimp, Listwire, iContact, Benchmark Email, Constant Contact, GetResponse, Vertical Response, Mad Mimi, GraphicMail, Emma.

TIP: Did you know that you can send 12,000 emails each month to up to 2,000 subscribers on *MailChimp* Forever Free Plan for absolutely no cost to you and only a MailChimp badge on your email footer?

35   Your Secret Weapon – A Dynamite Sign Up Form:

Your signup form should respond with two messages from you: the first welcomes the new subscriber, and the second has answers to the most popular questions about your site. These will be delivered automatically to subscribers when they sign up to your list.

Google *"Mad Libs" Style Form Increased Conversion by 25-40%* for details by Luke Wroblewski on a unique registration from at the Huffduffer site. It reads: I would like to use Huffduffer. I want **my username** to be [blank] and I want my **password** to be [blank]. My **email address** is [blank]. By the way, **my name** is [blank] and **my website** is [blank].

36 Signup form questions – Go for Gender, ZIP and Month of Birth:

One expert recommends limiting the number of questions on the sign up form to 3, including the email address. As for the others, he suggests gender, birthday (month and day) and ZIP code, because these pack the most punch for your promotion messages. If you go over 3 questions, you could lose replies (question fatigue?).

For a very good example of a sign up form and process, used by Ikea, Google *Step by Step: Ikea's Email Registration Process*. Note its friendly tone; the words "inspirational emails and updates"; the 5 fields in the sign up form, all mandatory, and the fact that you are then taken to a page that both confirms your sign up and asks additional questions; the size and clarity of the click boxes in the *get info that interests* you section.

Google *10 tips for better sign-up forms* by Mark Brownlow (where to locate the sign up form; allay privacy fears; tell them what they will get; tell them how often they will get it; give an example; get the right address; avoid jargon; get the email address first and then the infor-mation; test different forms).

TIP: *Reward for Sign Up* - Increase your signups to subscribe to your emails by giving readers *instant gratifi-cation* through a digital gift in the form of a PDF that adds value to your blog readers. Many free newsletters were signed up for because of free gifts.

Think of something that relates your Author Blog to something your readers will value, advises Rishi Shah, CEO of Digioh – an AWeber add-on that allows you to easily collect more email subscribers on your website. Google *Grow Your Email List With A Free Gift – And Digioh* for more details on how to design such a gift.

TIP: *Sign Up Gifts* - Brainstorm with your Team what kind of free gift might appeal to your Target Readers or Personas in return for their signing up to receive your emails or Newsletter.

Can you create a **webinar** in a subject you know some-thing about? Rishi Shah suggests this: "Record yourself talking about a favorite topic with a friend for an hour. Then listen to the recording and write it out. Presto magic – you just made your first PDF goodie!" You can upload your PDF or eBook gift to Digioh and get a link you can paste in your Author Blog or email header or autore-sponder signup confirmation email message.

Google *how to market your business with webinars AWeber* for an article on what webinars can do for you, the steps involved, the platforms to be used, the equipment you will need, the content requirements, and using email to deliver the webinars to your subscribers. Ambassadors; good webinars really add value when used as a reward for your readers.

37 Segmenting - Target your emails using Lists:

Segmentation is powerful if it gives you the chance to send relevant email messages to targeted subscribers rather than a one-size-fits-all broadcast to everyone. A message aimed at seniors could be different from one aimed at younger readers; messages incorporating geographic elements make more sense if they go to those subscribers in those areas, and so on.

One study showed that using email subscriber segmentation increased open and click rates by over 14%.

Space out your data mining efforts with your email subscribers, to avoid overload upfront. You can ask qualifying, narrowing questions about likes and dislikes, interests, content topic selection, demographs, other segmental information in a series of **_Getting to Know You_** quizzes.

38 Your Call to Action:

Did you make your call to action in your email as strong as you could? Does it fit what you want them to do (*Register today* if that is your aim; *Learn how to X* if it is your Newsletter)?

Use **_I'd Love Updates_** as the click point for your email subscribers to subscribe to your email list and Newsletter; sounds much better than Click Here.

39 Put your call-to-action above the fold –

Where you put your call-to-action can decide whether your email subscribers or blog readers click on it and respond. Should it be above or below the fold – the bottom of your reader's browser, the point they cannot see beyond. Aweber studies showed more clicks on the call-to-action if it was above the fold, but experiment with both.

40   Call to Action Brainstorming –

Brainstorm with your Team the types of calls to action you can include in your Email Plan.

What exactly do you want your readers to do? Why? What compelling reasons can you come up with to persuade them to do what you want them to do? What rewards (if any) will you give them if they do? What benefits will they receive, and how should you explain these to them? What action words should you use to trigger a response to your call for action? How have others used words to do this?

TIP: If you come across some good action words in calls to action by others in social networks, note them in your My Bloggy Book and discuss them with your Team. Will they work for you? Can you adapt them to make them work for you?

41   Three Homes for your Call to Action –

If you want readers to do something in response to your call to action (such as click through to your Author Blog post, or to a signup form for your Newsletter, or your Facebook page etc.), you can put your call to action in the *preheader* (that little line or two of small print just above the email header) or in the email *header* itself, or in the email *footer*. The more places they can respond, the higher the odds that they will. See the AWeber *Guide to User Friendly Emails* free download for details.

42   Action Words for your Calls to Action –

Liven up your email messages by spending time to infuse energy, excitement, and differentiation into some of the action words you use to draw attention to your calls for action.

The usual types of words include *add, arrange, buy, comment, own, reply, share, read, download, save,* and *consider.*

Now think about action words that wrap themselves around what *you* are doing.

You are a Rebel, an member of the Indie Community, an author on a Journey, an author who is building a Clan of Clan followers. So invite them to *Join the Revolution* by sharing a post that talks about the problems and benefits of self-publishing and the Indie Community. They can *Become a Rebel* by sharing a link to your Author Blog post about Indie Community challenges.

Or they can *Join-a-Tribe* by agreeing to become a signed up member of your Clan of Clan followers. Perhaps they *Wanna be an Ambassador?* and will join as one of your Brand Ambassadors. Or they might want to *Guide the Tribe* by sending you some tips or advice on how to engage your Target Readers.

If you ask them to *Flesh Them Out*, they might comment on the features of your Target Readers Personas.

So brainstorm ideas, try to be different, aim for engagement, freshness, and compulsion.

43   **Complete your Calls to Action –**

Sometimes a single word or two is not as good as a whole phrase that combines different elements of your Calls to Action. Experiment with different *combinations* so see what results in the most responses. Can you combine a powerful action word with a place and a compelling urgency and a deadline? And toss in a link as well? Try some powerful ***ComboCalls***.

Google *The 23 Best Lines in Marketing* for a list of action words you might use in your email messages (such as gift certificate enclosed; free offer inside; Thank you; What's new inside).

44   **Choose the right subject line for your emails:**

Is your email subject line less than 50 characters and urgent? Why not?

45   **Urgency & Relevance in your Subject Lines -**

Did you know that 1 out of 3 people dive into your email or click away to something else based only on what you put in the subject line of your email?

John Arnold in an article on *Designing the Subject Line for Your E-Mail Marketing Messages* on dummies.com points out that your subject line gives your readers a hint of the content of your email. If you want them to dive into the body of the email, that hint had better prompt them to look for specific information. He suggests you test your subject lines by sending two copies to a small sample (10%) of readers on your email list, and seeing which one works best.

Arnold says your subject line should have 2 things immediately apparent: *urgency* and *relevance.*

The subject line should clearly state the *immediate benefit to the reader of opening the message* (shades of instant gratification!). The immediacy of the benefit makes your email seem urgent and leads to the opening of the message.

He recommends using words that your readers associate with relevant (to them) information. Think of your Personas: what is relevant to them in your message?

46   The From Line of your Emails:

Arnold says you want your From line to reassure your reader that you are trustworthy and the email worth opening; many readers click in or click away based on who is sending the email. So getting them to stay to consider your subject line starts with them accepting you in the From line.

How do you do that? You should decide how your readers are most likely to recognize you, and build a From line that gives them what they need. Your From line should have your name, if that is the most recognizable thing about you (if your Author Brand they have been exposed to is based on your name), or your book (if that is the most recognizable thing about you).

47   Keep your email short:

What length should your emails be? Variety is the spice of life here, too, but the general rule is short, punchy messages, with no more than 3 or 4 items.

Instead of sending one long email, try chunking it by breaking it into shorter emails, with links to the other emails in the series.

You can cut a long email down by using summaries with links to the fuller articles elsewhere (in your blog posts or Newsletter). You can also shorten the email but keep it punchy by throwing in a short extract of the longer article with a link to your blog or Newsletter.

48   Content is King for emails:

TIP: Download MailChimp's free *Email Marketing A MailChimp Field Guide* for some practical and helpful hints on best email marketing practices.

49   *How often should you send emails to new subscribers?* –

Google *What Intervals Does AWeber Suggest For Messages* for their suggested intervals between email messages to new subscribers. More often in the beginning; fewer later on. First one to be sent automatically when they sign up; second 1 to 2 days later; third 3 to 4; fifth 4 to 9, then 5 to 15, then 9 to 30, then 30 plus days.

50   Using your email lists for a drip marketing campaign:

Go to this site for a video that introduces the concept of a drip marketing campaign:

http://www.pinpointe.com/blog/drip-marketing-campaign-tips

Drip marketing is just what is says: the steady drip-drip-drip of marketing messages to prospects over time, using your email autoresponders to set the triggers for the messages.

Your drip marketing campaign should be carefully planned, and you need to really think through the messages you wish to send. It is a good way to build awareness of you and your books, and should work well with promoting new books in your series of books. It is also a way to make your Author Brand jell in your subscribers minds.

It is also a good means to provide items of educational value to the recipients, so using it for targeted value-added articles aimed at the known interests of the subscribers works.

The risk is that it is seen as impersonal, offensive and boring, and if badly handled could lead to losing subscriptions.

Brainstorm your drip marketing campaign themes with your Team.

Drip campaigns are often used for *set and forget* campaigns that provide for automatic product trial downloads, or for *customer nurturing* programs. You could prepare separate value-added messages (such as downloadable rewards as PDFs with functioning hyperlinks to other sites of value to the recipients) which only go out to those subscribers on your lists who agreed to receive your messages geared to their specified interests. This means those who want it, get it, and those who did not want it, are not offended.

Some triggers for your drip marketing campaign - These could include a simple reminder to your listed subscribers; adding people to a new list at some future date; add them to a list when they click a link in your campaign; or other triggers.

51   Your very own email (digital) Newsletter:
Your Newsletter lets you deliver news about your journey as an author, any promotions you might have, and other time-sensitive content. Use your Newsletter to let your readers know who you are; telling them about your journey as an Indie publisher – with humor – will add a face to the Newsletter.

52   Why do people like Newsletters? –
Because they meet one or more of the 3 main needs of people who use social networks (entertainment; nurturing their friends; or learning); because they love to follow the breadcrumbs of teasers to find the pot full of honey at its end; because they can participate in a macrologue with other readers of the Newsletter.

Your aim is to have such value-added content in your Newsletter that your readers share it with their friends.

TIP: Google *Create Effective Email Newsletters AWeber* for a free **webinar** on this topic, covering using their Broadcast tool to create Newsletters, content ideas and scheduling and formatting tips for such Newsletters.

53   Newsletter link –
If you link to an example of your Newsletter in the signup form, potential subscribers can check out exactly what they will be getting if they sign up; adds credibility to your suggestion that they subscribe to the Newsletter.

54   Forwarded Newsletters –
Capitalize on any subscriber forwarding your web versions of your Newsletter to their friends by adding a

subscriber signup form to your Newsletter; the friend can immediately sign up to get it directly. If you don't make it easy for them to do so, you might lose the chance to gain another subscriber.

55   Engagement with email subscribers –

Brainstorm with your Team the many ways you can go about making your digital Newsletter more valuable to your subscribers by asking subscribers for their suggestions on the content of your Newsletter. Ask them what problems they face, and how you and your contributors to the Newsletter can help solve them.

56   Use Multiple Newsletters through a variety opt-in process–

Think about using more than one digital Newsletter for your email subscribers, sending the right one to the right email subscriber based on their choice from your menu of options based on interests. Use the same framework for each version, with similar topics but certain parts targeted at the interests chosen.

57   Newsletter keywords –

Ask your potential newsletter subscribers what keywords they use when searching for topics of interest to them, then see if you can use common keywords in your content, and choose topics dealing with those keywords.

58   Timeliness –

Take pains to make your email and digital Newsletter content both timely and relevant, because many of your subscribers look to Newsletters to stay ahead of the curve.

How often should you publish your digital Newsletter? Start off slowly – Small Steps with Small Wins – by doing it once a month, then later on try once every two weeks or once a week.

TIP: *Backlink your Newsletter & Author Blog posts –* Embed into each article links to other sources of related information in your social networks, such as similar posts in past issues of the Newsletter or in past blog posts.

59 Great expectations & Newsletter Sneak Peeks –

If your potential Newsletters can actually read a copy before they sign up to get it, the chances of them signing up are much, much greater. Instead of buying a pig in a poke, they know what to expect.

In AWeber you do this by combining your broadcast archive of your Newsletters with the web form generator and so sneak peeks are possible.

Web versions of your past broadcast messages of your Newsletters are stored in your AWeber broadcast archive and the web form generator allows you to create custom signup forms where readers can subscribe to your emails. You simply display a Direct Link in your web signup form to the archived version of one of your Newsletters.

60 Newsletter: Calling the Clan –

Add a Calling the Clan section to your Newsletter once you have a few readers who have indicated they would like to join your Clan. Add a few messages to the Clan in this portion of the Newsletter.

61   Newsletter: Advice from Indies –

Once you've joined or formed your Writers Club, ask them for some advice for Indie Community members and drop these into your Advice from Indies portion of your Newsletter.

62   Newsletter: Indie Stories –

In this section of your Newsletter, add stories by members of the self-publishing Indie Community about their own experiences in publishing, their problems and challenges on their own journeys. Add their photos and potted bios, if they agree.

63   Add tips to your email messages:

Adding tips to your Newsletter adds oomph to each edition, IF you have thought about the kind of tips your Target Reader Personas want or could use, AND you have gathered the tips carefully, making sure that each tip adds value to the readers. Add links to the source of the tip, and let people know what you think about the tips.

64   Use email to announce your Twitter, Author Blog and Amazon Author Page:

It's a good way to make these announcements, and to drive some interest to them.

Other TIPS for promoting your book using email:

65   Split testing –

You use split testing with your broadcast messages to find out which of two messages works best in terms of openings and link clicking. In AWeber the QuickStats feature allows you to check how each test message worked.

66   Summary –

Experiment by testing new subject lines, checking what is working best, finding out what kind of content results in the most click-throughs, segmenting your subscriber list, and trying different calls to action.

67   Personas Feedback –

Can you identify common problems facing your various Personas? If you can, you can write blog posts or Newsletter articles on how to solve these problems, and give feedback by email to your subscribers every time you post.

68   Feedback –

Add a rating scale at the bottom of each blog broadcast for feedback from readers (scales show boring to very useful etc.)

69   Rating of Campaign –

Get feedback from your readers on your promotional campaigns by posing a question below the messages about how effective they think it is, typing Not Useful then the numbers 1 to 5 and then Very Useful.

By linking each number to a *Thank You Page* on your Author Blog, they can give you feedback very easily.

Your Thank You Page post can itself be used to alert your readers that you will be seeking feedback from them every now and then.

The AWeber *click tracking* feature will let you find out how often each link is clicked.

70 **First email autoresponder message** –

Nick Moore of AWeber suggests having these in your first autoresponder message to subscribing readers so as to maximize the opportunity you have with freshly signed up subscribers:

- confirm they were successfully signed up to receive your emails;
- then thank them for signing up;
- if you offered a free bonus for signing up use this chance to deliver it;
- remind them how they will benefit from your messages;
- tell them what to expect.

71 **Your Autorespond series of messages** –

Pace yourself; prepare a series of autorespond messages to be used when a subscriber signs up to receive your emails. Space them out, and have 2 to 5 prepared.

72 **Gamification and Your Email Plan:**

Gamification means using games to increase a user's engagement with something. It's a fairly recent development in business, based on the wild popularity of traditional digital games.

The techniques used in gamifiying a non-game business proposal are these:

Rewards –

You do what I want you to do and at each level you get a reward, such as points, achievement badges (think about the Amazon Reviewers levels and badges – see 10.1 and 10.2), a visible progress bar showing where you are, of more recently giving you virtual money that you can spend on the site.

Competition –

Let everybody see how you are progressing, and you will try harder; using leader boards that show the rankings is one way to do this.

Use games –

Build games into the tasks you want done on your site (give them a meaningful choice or an increasing challenge, and add a story about what is going on).

Does it work? Do you think going from a 10% success rate to an 80% one is a success?

Google *devhub gets users hooked by gamifying its service* for the story of how DevHub, which provides software for users to build their own websites, pushed the success rate of their users up from 10% who finished their websites to a whopping 80%, using game mechanics on their site to reward their users with points, coins and badges. If you added more features to your website or blog, you got these rewards.

DevHub created levels of site completion, and you went up a level if you finished one of the step-by-step additions to your site.

Think about how you can on your own use some of the gamification techniques to increase opt ins to your email and Newsletter.

Reward gamification & Tasks linkage in your social network meta-game:

You should as a first step consider using the concept of a **meta-game**, which an umbrella that ties mini-games or games mechanics together into one whole.

Instead of just thinking of one-off rewards to your readers, such as issuing a value-added white paper to someone who signed your email subscription opt-in form, use linkage: ask the reader to do three things, each with a reward of its own, and measure all three tasks in a dashboard on your blog site.

What could those linked tasks be?

Things like sharing a blog post with a number of friends; or joining your Clan of Clan followers; or Liking specific Facebook posts; or sending the email subscription opt-in form to a set number of friends along with their recommendation that the friends opt-in; or reading a certain thread on the Amazon or Kindle or some other Forum, and contributing their own comments to it; or commenting on your named blog posts; or entering their own photos into your monthly themed Facebook photo competition; or providing you with suggestions for further engagement methods with your readers, or completing a survey or information gathering quiz you set up.

Later on you can take a second step, by offering rewards such as points, coins or some other digital currency for tasks taken by your readers. They can use the digital currency to unlock various rewards.

I would not be surprised to see simpler gamification plugins developed for author blogs in the near future.

Rewards & Engagement –

Try to match your Rewards to the level of engagement of your readers, because research has shown that we are happier when we earn something, rather than when it is given to us.

Crank them up: the more engaged they are, the bigger the Rewards. Use gamification as your example!

Gamification – Hints:

If you plan to use gamification techniques to reward and engage your readers, add these elements to it:

- Points (show them how they are doing);
- Badges (from easy to tough to earn);
- Levels (earn you way up to a higher level through some social equity – read: sweat equity – your readers have spent, such as comments on your Blog or Facebook, retweeting your tweets, signing up readers, signing up people to join your Clan of Clan followers);
- Leaderboards (to rank their efforts); and
- Challenges (which might require group play by your readers).

73   Personalize Your Readers:

TIP: *Personalize your Readers* – Reach out via email to them to participate in your ***About My Readers*** posts to your social networks (your Author Blog, your digital Newsletter, your Facebook page) showing their photos and short bios about them and their interests.

Brand Advocacy and Brand Ambassador:

74   Invite brand advocacy from your Readers –

Ask your readers for their views and comments on how your content might have helped them, and use those in later posts in your social networks (your Author Blog, your Newsletter, your email messages). This leverages off brand advocacy, which is a recommendation of a brand (your Brand Touch messages) by a peer group member.

Google *9 Reasons Your Company Should Use Brand Advocates: New Research* for a good article by *socialmediaexaminer* on how to do enroll your email subscribers as your *Brand Ambassadors*.

75   Your Brand Advocates –

Ask your email subscribers if they would like to become your brand advocates (i.e. your Brand Ambassadors).

A *brand advocate* is any customer who has been officially commissioned to speak on behalf of your brand without compensation.

Note that asking your readers if they would like to become your brand advocates or Brand Ambassadors might satisfy one of the 3 major needs that I believe people who use social networks have (entertainment; nurturing their friends; or learning).

The above study found that 54% of brand advocates or brand influencers viewed the sharing of information as a type of relaxation, and were 83% more likely to share information with others. <u>Brand advocates value being seen as reliable sources of information.</u>

If they decide to become your Brand Ambassador, ***show them the luv***: their relationship with you, according to the study, is important to them and they need to know that you value their friendship as part of the mutual exchange in the relationship.

Google *20 ways to succeed at social media engagement* by salesforceradian6 for hints on your best engagement methods.

TIP: Sign up for regular emails from http://www.socialmediaexaminer.com/ to help guide you through your social media jungle.

76   **Video of book extracts –**

Add videos of people reading passages from your book to your promotion messages (emails, blog posts, Facebook page entries). Use different friends, or invite your Clan followers and Brand Ambassadors to record them and send them to you for your (free) use. Perhaps arrange a competition among your Brand Ambassadors, all reading the same passage, with your readers voting for the Top 3?

TIP: Google *Corralling Email Content to Create Value* by Chris Studabaker for some handy points on how to marshal content in your email messages, your Newsletter, and your Author Blog posts.

77   **Stories as Content –**

A succession of emails can end up boring, so liven them up with the story of your journey as an Indie member: your trials and tribulations, your minor victories, your recent small steps and small wins, your discussions with your

Team, your methods to find topics to talk about – the list is endless. Oh, and add a dash of emotion!

78   Guest experts –

Invite your email subscribers to try out to become a guest expert on aspects of writing and of the Indie book promotion. They would have to become a Brand Ambassador for you to qualify. You would post their contributions on your Author Blog; posts should be short and punchy, and you would reserve the right to edit them. A photo of your Guest Expert could also be used, if they agree.

79   Spam filters and attachments –

Most spam filters on servers will have problems with attachments, so handle them very carefully. Don't use them unless you have to.

80   Tone –

Use a friendly tone in emails to make your readers connect more personally with you. AWeber advises: have a real conversation with your customers. Experiment with different tones to see what works best with what Personas.

Use a real address – Not any *noreply* addresses (which rob the mail of any personal touch).

81   Anniversary –

Celebrate the anniversary of the date the subscriber joined you with an email; AWeber can automate this for you. Can you give them a download digital reward?

82   Evergreen content –

Keep even automated follow ups fresh by using ever-green content of value to your subscribers. If you get frequent questions about anything (comments on your Author Blog, discussions with friends, responses on threads in forums etc.), prepared answers and use these.

As you create your automated follow ups, focus on content that customers will find useful for a long time to come. Marcus Sheridan – an entrepreneur, small business marketer and AWeber customer – recommends paying attention to the questions your customers frequently ask, along with the search terms that bring the most traffic to your web site. Address these questions in your automated campaign for content that will feel fresh and relevant for customers who sign up now or a year from now.

83   Repurposed content –

Remember the *Three Bites Rule* and make sure each and every Brand Touch message or article or product you create has at least 3 use through reworking (as tutorials, printed articles used for email messages, etc.).

84   What works? –

Your open and click through rates will tell you how much your subscribers appreciate your content of individual messages: how often they open your emails and how often they click through to your site content. Try different things to see what changes the open and click through rates.

85   Link your archive to Facebook –

Link your broadcast archive to your Facebook status page so Facebook viewers can access past emails or Newsletters you sent out (recycling them). As the Newsletter has an email signup form, your Facebook viewers can easily sign up as subscribers to your Newsletter.

TIP: Download the free pdf *Guide to User Friendly Emails* available on the AWeber site for many good, practical hints on drafting effective emails.

86   Let your preheader summarize the email

In a line or two, explain gist of the email; this can be helpful if the reader has images switched off.

87   Please share this –

You might encourage sharing of your emails with readers' friends by adding a in the footer or the preheader of the email a *Forward to a Friend* link (see AWeber's *Guide to User Friendly Emails* free download for details).

88   Give your subscribers choices –

Add a link in your email preheader or email footer to a link to an Edit Preferences page; this allows your email subscribers to make choices about several things: choose getting your emails less often or more often; change their email address; choose from a menu of topics they want to get emails from you about. This gives your subscribers autonomy and shows you care about their comfort.

See AWeber's *Guide to User Friendly Emails* free pdf download on their site for more details.

In the choose topics portion, consider adding a choice of one or all of special digital studies or reports or articles you have drafted for your Target Readers. You can update these choices at later times for new rewards to your readers.

89   Unsubscribe link in email preheader –

Consider putting the link to the unsubscribe decision (called Unsubscribe) in your email preheader so subscribers can see it easily.

TIP: If you use a preheader for your email different from your subject line, and provide something useful to subscribers in these one or two lines of smaller text of a lighter color than your main text, you might improve the chances of them opening your email (see AWeber's free pdf download *Guide to User Friendly Emails* for more details). Try teasers to tempt them to read the whole email.

TIP: Add as a Task to your Promotion Plan, sessions with your Team during which you go through all the Tips in this book to see which ones you should use, when, and how.

TIP: Add a link to your Amazon Author Page in your email preheader, so that your email subscribers can check your book covers, book reviews, your author details and your book descriptions whenever they get an email from you.

90   Link your Emails to your Hub –

Add a link in your email preheader (in small print) directly to your Author Blog, the hub of your Author Platform. See AWeber's free pdf download of *Guide to User Friendly Emails* for details.

91 *Add a Navigation Guide to your email preheader* –

Adding a navigation bar with 2 to 5 links to your email header allows your subscribers to go directly to the sites linked to; these could be your Author Blog; a web copy of your Newsletter in your broadcast archive; your Facebook page etc.

See AWeber's free pdf download of *Guide to User Friendly Emails* for details.

92 **Email header links** –

You can add links in your email header to other sites, such as Manage Email Preferences, or your Author Blog, or Forward to a Friend etc. See AWeber's free pdf download of *Guide to User Friendly Emails* for details.

93 **Email footer** –

Add your valid physical postal address if your email is a commercial one, as required by the U.S. CAN-SPAM Act in your footer; also consider your unsubscribe link and social sharing icons (Facebook, Twitter); or navigation links. See AWeber's free pdf download *Guide to User Friendly Emails*.

TIP: Add user-friendly links in your email preheader, header or footer to increase the friendliness and helpfulness of your emails.

94 **Blog broadcast to email subscribers** –

You can arrange for your Author Blog posts to be sent automatically to the email address of your email subscribers using AWeber's blog broadcast feature.

You choose how many days elapse between blog broadcasts, or on what days of the week they should be sent.

TIP: Google *How do I create a Blog Broadcast* for the detailed AWeber instructions.

95   Link your email message to your Author & Book Videos –

If you embed a video directly into an email, your email will be nixed as spam by most servers. But you *can* link to a page on your Author Blog that has the Author or Book Video (or any other permitted video) embedded in it.

Your link can be a hyperlinked keyword or keywords for HTML messages, or the full URL address for Plain Text email messages.

96   Subscriber information in your email footer –

Add subscriber details to your footer (name, date subscribed, email address) plus ability to change subscription – Google *Why Personalize My Messages* for AWeber how-to instructions.

97   How can you personalize your emails? –

AWeber allows you to personalize your messages by using a variety of variables (including: subscribers name, email address, signup date, subscriber location taken from his or her IP address – country, region, city).

Google *What is Personalization* by Nick Moore for discussion.

98 Attachments & Digioh:

Often many Internet service providers will not allow any e-mails through that are larger than 2MB or if allowed through it will fill the users e-mail box.

Can I send attachments with my emails? –

Gmail, Yahoo! Mail, Hotmail, Outlook and Mail allow you to send attachments; the paperclip icon is the one to use. However, may Internet service providers (ISPs) limit the size of email attachments to 2MB so as to prevent filling recipients' email boxes. Google *send large files to other people outlook* for a discussion of alternative methods for sending large files, and see below for using AWeber and AWeber plus Digioh to do so.

Can I send attachments with my emails using AWeber? –

AWeber allows you to attach up to one megabyte (1 MB) to your email message. You can use this to send PDFs and other small files to subscribers – such as the digital rewards you prepared as described in 6.4 above.

What if my attachment is bigger than the 1 MB AWeber allows? –

If you want to send bigger file, consider placing that file on a page in your website or blog site with a link in your email to that page. Or you can sign up to **Digioh**, a digital download service AWeber has an association with, to send larger files. Google *How Do I Send Attachments to Messages?* for AWeber's article on this. And Google *Grow Your Email List with a Free Gift – And Digioh* for some ideas.

TIP: If you write a post for another blogger as a guest blogger, consider adding the **Digioh** link to that post along with a freebie (PDF etc.) to attract readers of that other blog to become your email subscribers.

*What does **Digioh** charge for sending attachments to my email subscribers? –*

Digioh has a free service but it is limited (only one file, with a maximum of 10 transactions and a maximum file size of 50MB). Digioh's paid services costs US$14.99 a month (at February 2013) and has unlimited downloads, 10 files and a maximum file size of 500 MB.

*What services does **Digioh** provide me? –*

It provides you with a link that you include in your email to subscribers so they can click on it to download your digital files. Digioh lets you keep track of which subscribers downloaded what products, when and how many times; this shows you which subscribers are most interested in the product you offered and you can use that information for a follow-up email to them, or to segment your subscriber list.

Can I send attachments to my email subscribers with MailChimp? –

No; you need to upload your document or PDF to MailChimp and then link to the file in your emails. This does not meet everyone's needs and does not give you any analytics about who downloads etc. MailChimp has integrated **Digioh**, just as AWeber has. Google *mailchimp digioh* for details.

*Can I include **clickable hyperlinks** in my PDF documents I send to my email subscribers? –*

NovaPDF (see 2.13 above for more details) results in clickable hyperlinks in your PDFs which your email subscribers will be able to click on and go to the sites hyperlinked to. Many programs that create PDFs do not allow this. If your gift or reward to your subscribers is, say, a list of good blog posts on a topic you selected, you need to be able to make your hyperlinks clickable.

TIP: Go here for AWeber tutorials on how to manage an effective email subscription campaign: http://blog.aweber.com/videos

TIP: Google *Creating And Hosting Your Own Webinar AWeber* for a free webinar by AWeber on how to do exactly that. Covers recommendations for hardware and software to make webinars, which are seminars offered over the Web, and how to set up and prep for your own webinar, and also integrate your email campaign with your own webinar.

99   Using Stair-Stepping Emails:

You use a stair-stepping email structure to save the time of your busy email subscribers, because it allows them to decide what to do after reading your most important message in your email. You put the most important message first in the email, so they see it first; then they can choose to go to the other parts of the message, on the lower stairs. The font size of those lower stairs is smaller than the first stair. AWeber tests show that the lower down the stairs a link is, the fewer clicks it will get. Google *marketing email pattern #2: stair stepping* for more details

TIP: Google *guerilla marketing for small businesses: repurposing content* for an article on how to use the same work in many different ways, on many different launching platforms (the 3 bites rule).

100   Content Forms and Platforms for Repurposed:

An example (showing 9 content form types followed by the platform used to launch each form in brackets) is: Blog post (Blogger is the platform); video (YouTube); presentation (Slideshare); webinar (GoToWebinar); infographic (Visual.ly); podcast (iTunes); press release (PRWeb); email (AWeber); and social media (Facebook).

TIP: Google *grow your email list 99% faster: how one site did it* to read how using **popup or lightbox form** to recruit signups did exactly that, then consider experimenting with it for your emails. An Aweber customer found that using a pop-over sign for his opt-in form and delaying the time it appeared based on the average amount of time visitors spent on his site (he found 60 second delay worked for him), significantly increased his opt-ins. There did not seem to be any annoyance at the pop-over sign.

101   Surveys to boost your engagement levels –

Use the free *surveymonkey* survey to question your readers and increase their engagement. SurveyMonkey has 30 million people taking their surveys each month.

The free version means you agree to getting emails from SurveyMonkey. You can add the survey to your Facebook Page with their app. You use 15 different question types, including demographic questions and customer feedback questions. You can post it on Facebook, or use Twitter, or by emails to your email subscribers.

Google *how to survey your customers and prospects aweber* for an article explaining how you can use Google Docs, the free online suite of word processing and software, to create forms in your Google spreadsheets. So you can create your form (your spreadsheet will automatically be created for you), and email the link to your email subscribers through AWeber. They respond to the email without having to sign in, and the responses are automatically added to your spreadsheet.

Google *Create Surveys to Segment Your Subscribers: 5 Steps AWeber* for an article with useful suggestions about the types of questions to ask to segment your subscribers, and how to analyze the results and then divide your subscribers into segments for further action (targeted emails, follow up questions, value-added content, windows for sending out emails etc.).

You can build in **rating scales** into your AWeber emails to gauge how much your subscribers like your emails, Newsletters, Author Blog posts etc.. Google *do subscribers like your emails? Ask! AWeber* for an article on how to do this.

Google *9 Ways You Can Get To Know Your Subscribers Better AWeber* for a good grouping of ways you can use AWeber to flesh out your knowledge of your email subscribers to improve your engagement triggers.

Once you have a big enough email subscriber list, considering asking your Clan followers if they have any questions they might wish to add to your regular polls or surveys; don't forget to identify them as the source of the question.

102   Clarify the Journey:

Experiment with your Author Blog (your landing site), and your email forms, to answer this question: Is the journey you want your email subscribers to take very clearly set out for them?

Your goal with your emails is to not make a sale, but to earn a click to a landing page that will try to make a sale. Your Author Blog is the hub of your promotion channels and it should give your subscribers all the reasons they need to move from first glance to decision to purchase your book, or download your rewards or value-added content, or fill out a survey form designed to improve your Brand Touches.

Add value to your Newsletters by including a section *Ask Me* and then calling for questions from your readers, with you giving the answers. Personalize the *Ask Me* section by including a short bio of each reader, along with his or her photo.

103   Cross-Pollinating with your Newsletter –

Include links in your Newsletters to posts in your Author Blog (as well as earlier articles in the Newsletter itself).

104   Newsletter as your Loyalty Driver –

Newsletters offer a better chance than simple emails to cement the loyalty of recipients. IF you have added the right kind and quantity of value for your Newsletter readers. One way to test this is to experiment with different types of articles. Another is to ask them.

105 What to call them? –

Ask your Newsletter recipients what they would prefer to be called. Offer a menu of words, including one that might top the others: **Member**. We all like to belong, and being addressed as a Member rather than by the more sterile word Subscriber makes for a more personal relationship with you. Test Clan Member (from your Clan of Clan followers).

106 Social Proof through a Testimonial Video & Subscriber Counter:

Sometimes a link to a video with a testimonial from a satisfied subscriber works wonders by adding social proof to the request for a sign up from a subscriber.

Once you have a large enough number of subscribers, consider using a *subscriber counter*, starting at the large enough number, as a social proof demonstration. If so many others subscribe, why don't I?

AWeber has a subscriber count chicklet that you can add to the AWeber opt-in form to show your visitors how many others read your Newsletter.

Do a split-test with and without it to find out if it boosts your conversion rate. **An AWeber customer in 2008 increased opt-ins by 32% using the chicklet**. The subscriber count sits below the opt-in form and says simply *X readers*. Adding the chicklet to the opt-in form is simple; you click a Counter button on top of the web form editor and it's done.

107 Headlines –

Experiment with a headline that is personal, or curious; avoid the impression you are selling something.

Try repeating your message several times in the body of the email – remember: we all skim emails, so we might miss it the first time round. Try wording it a bit differently.

TIP: Rewarding your readers can take the form of a Thank You post in your Author Blog that includes links to other bloggers that you think will be useful to your segmented readers. It could meet one of their three top needs from social networks ((entertainment; nurturing their friends; or learning).

TIP: *Low-key your sales pitch or die* – Most of us just really really really don't want a pitch made to us by some stranger on the phone, nor do we want a hard pitch made to us via email.

So double check every email message you send out to take out the hard pitches. Make it indirect; better still, don't make it. Let your Author Brand show through, and the value in your content lead them to your books, rather than a hard sell.

You can stick helpful headlines in many places in your email messages. Main headlines. Paragraph headlines and subheadings. Captions under your images. Navigation links. Use Headlines that Hook.

TIP: Check this dummies.com article on basic marketing principles for email marketing:

http://www.dummies.com/how-to/content/using-basic-marketing-principles-with-email-market.html

Make it easy to scan your emails by adding white space and guides for the eyes.

Don't forget to greet your readers, and thank them in a short goodbye sentence.

108 Gifts & Others' Email Lists –

For one view of how to "shower" gifts upon readers so that they "lend" you their own email lists to offer gifts to their addressees and coordinate purchases of your Amazon book on the same day and hopefully drive up your ranking, *Google Getting Your Book to #1 at Amazon* and *Jason Oman.* He includes the types of gifts offered and the email asking to use the lists of recipients.

Google *The Essentials of Building Your E-Mail Marketing Lists* for the series by www.dummies.com.

1   What is Listmania?

This is what Amazon says it is:

Listmania Lists include products you find interesting. Maybe there's a short stack of books you always keep at your bedside, albums you'd want to take to a desert island, or a "kit" of various things--manuals, computer peripherals, instructional videos--that helped you start a home business. You don't need to have purchased these items from Amazon.com.

The opinions expressed in Listmania lists are the opinions of Amazon.com customers and not necessarily the opinions of Amazon.com.

So Listmania allows you to create a list of up to 40 of your favorite books, around a common theme, and to include your own book along with those of your competitors. All books you choose must be listed on Amazon but do not need to be Kindle eBooks.

Any List can be sorted by clicking *Sort By* and then your choice, such as *Last Updated* on the bottom of the results page.

2   Why should you use Listmania?

Like birds of a feather that stick together, Listmania Lists benefit from the company they keep, and you choose that company.

You should choose the most popular books in the same genre (Category, Keywords) of your book, and add them to your Lists, so that hopefully some of their popularity will spill over and benefit your book – popularity by associa-tion.

Your own book should be at the top of your Listmania List.

Every time a reader searches for one of the popular books you have added to your own List, your List might appear in a side panel along with that book.

Amazon examines all the Lists to decide which ones to use with which books. Your chances of someone being intrigued by your own increases if readers checking other books of the same genre find your List placed next to that book.

Your Lists would also be searchable by Google and oth-er search engines.

3 How does Listmania work?

Creating your own Listmania List is easy.

On your Profile Page you click Edit Your Profile, then Lists in the Contributions section, then Create your first one now and provide the information Amazon asks for. Google *amazon profile page* to find out what that is (it is not your Amazon Author).

That information is also simple: you need a name for your List; to describe your qualifications to show why you are an expert on the List subject and why others should bother to read your List; an introduction to describe the List; and the Products (the books, with your own book at the top of your List).

Voila! You are now a Listmaniac!

4 Where do you find Amazon's Lists?

Google *How to find Listmania Lists (7 steps) ehow.*

And Google *Listmania lists* plus your topic such as *horror*, and you will find Lists on that topic.

Or use this Google customized search (just the topic, such as *horror*, in the panel):

https://www.google.com/cse/home?cx=017986067167 581999535:4-ekn3oenek

5   Amazon's Guidelines for Listmania:

Amazon's Participation Guidelines apply to Listmania Lists. The general guidelines are simple: no nastiness, no phone numbers or URLs, no prices, no soliciting for external Web sites.

6   How to create your own Lists for Listmania:

Here are some Hooks for you to consider when drawing up your own Lists:

***Headline Hooks* –**

The same principle apply here – make your List names stand out and grab attention.

***Qualification Hook* –**

Use your *Author Brand Elevator Speech* for consistency when describing who you are and why you are qualified to make your List.

***Benefits Hook* –**

This goes into the Introduction paragraph and explains why a reader will benefit from reading your List. What's in it for each of your Target Reader Personas? How can they use your List? Who can they send it to if it is a useful list (they switch into your Brand Ambassadors each time they do something like this)?

TIPS on how to use Listmania:

7   Collect Lists:

Add the titles (headlines) of Listmania Lists you find eye-catching to your *My **Bloggy Book*** for later use when you are brainstorming with your Team titles for your next set of Lists.

8   Use more than one List:

Don't just use one List.

Include as one of the tasks in your Small Steps Plan writing a List to upload to Amazon at regular intervals, perhaps one every two weeks or even every week.

9   Match your Lists to your Personas:

Brainstorm with your Team to create a separate Listmania List for each one of your Target Reader Personas, to allow for fruitful cross-pollination.

10   Use Cooperative Lists:

Experiment with your own Lists after checking the Lists of others.

Consider cooperating with other Indie Community authors, and your Clan members, to come up with shared lists etc.

Or do a post on your Writers Club's selection of The Top [10][20] Listmania List Titles (do it monthly, and consider breaking it down by genre).

11   Add Value with your Lists:

Make sure that each of your Lists does indeed benefit your target readers (your Lists are one of your many Author Brand Touches).

12   Piggyback the Bestsellers in your Lists:

Make a point of adding some blockbuster Super seller books in your own Lists – harness their pulling power to bring readers to your own books.

13   Ride the Trends with your Listmania Lists:

Practice the art of **Trend Riding** when choosing blockbusters and other books for your own Listmania Lists, so that your Lists are fresh and topical!

Google *33 free trend tracking tools* and select those dealing with Amazon books.

Try to be among the very first List makers to collect books dealing with a trend and add them to your own List (assuming your own book has a theme, or locale, or character, or plot angle, or some attribute that fits in with the trend you want to ride).

Combine your trendy Lists with posts in your Author Blog and Tweets etc.

You can also *anticipate trends* by planning ahead for events that will happen and compiling lists adding value to readers interested in those events just before they happen or when they take place, for e.g.: elections, seasons, school terms, deadlines such as tax deadlines etc.

14   Use your own Ranking Lists:

You can add a twist to your own Listmania Lists by prioritizing the books you have read and wish to use in your

List according to various criteria (e.g.: My favorites in order; ranking of 10 (15? 20?) books on Kennedy chosen by [my Clan members] [my Indie Community cooperative author group]; or ranked by detailed description of [this event, person] and so on). This can add qualitative value to your Lists.

15   Tell them you have Listed them:

Let the authors know on their block sites or via Twitter you have included their book in your own Listmania List (with links to your Author Blog).

1   Your 4 Kinds of Book Reviews:

You will be looking for reviews of your book from 5 different kinds of reviewers: your own Editorial Review; Amazon Customer Reviews; Amazon's stable of book reviewers; and non-Amazon book reviewers.

Book reviews are a very important *recommendation and media shopping tools* that you need to use in order to migrate your book up from the thin end of the Long Tail of products on Amazon, towards the Head.

2   Your own Editorial Review:

Google *amazon editorial review of books* to find Amazon's rules for your own review or your own book. It appears in your book's Product Detail Page, and must be recorded as being From the Author. Your own editorial review is limited to 600 characters. Use your Book Elevator Speech as part of your own review.

3   Amazon Customer Reviews:

Reviews of your book written by customers of Amazon are found near the bottom of the product detail page of your book. <u>Amazon does not control customer reviews, so you are at the mercy of your readers</u>.

Seeking such reviews would be one of the tasks in your Small Steps Plan. Before a customer can post such a review, he or she must have an Amazon.com account that has been charged for the purchase of ANY physical or digital item (free digital downloads do NOT qualify);

HOWEVER the customer does NOT have to purchase your book in order to review it.

4   Amazon's Stable of Book Reviewers:

Amazon has a list of thousands of unpaid reviewers who do not work for Amazon.

See below for more information on these Amazon top reviewers. They are a prime target for the book review part of your Small Steps Plan.

5   Non-Amazon Book Reviewers:

There are thousands of other book reviewers who review books for the fun of it, and a small number who expect to be paid to do so. See below for more information on this category of book reviewers. They are also prime targets for your book review part of your Small Steps Plan.

6   Amazon Policy on Paid Book Reviews:

The Amazon policy regarding paid reviews seems to be that paid reviews are welcome in your own Editorial Reviews section of your book's detail page, but are not allowed in the Customer Review's section unless such compensation is ONLY a free copy of the book being reviewed.

Here's Amazon's guidelines:

"Can I pay for someone to write a Customer Review for my book?

No. We don't allow any form of compensation for a Customer Review <u>other than a free copy of the book provided upfront</u>. If you offer a free advanced copy, it must be clear that you welcome all feedback, both positive and negative. If we detect that a customer was paid to write a review, we'll remove it. **The only type of paid review that Amazon supports is an editorial review**. An editorial review is a more formal evaluation of a book usually written by an editor or expert within a genre, but can also be written by family and friends. If you've received an editorial review of your book that you'd like to post to the Editorial Review section of your book's detail page, please visit our Author Central Help Page."

Make one of your tasks in your Small Steps Plan arranging for paid editorial reviews according to the rules, by an "editor or expert within a genre" or by your friends (Brand Ambassadors who are good reviewers?).

7   Reviews by Sock-Puppets:

Note that Amazon has advised some writers that reviews by other authors may not be made, as Amazon does "not allow reviews on behalf of a person or company with a financial interest in the product or a directly competing product. This includes authors, artists, publishers, manufacturers, or third-party merchants selling the product".

So if any other author has a financial interest in your book, or in their own book and it is a "competing product" (whatever that means – the same genre as your book? Or just another book of any genre?) their review of your book would be disallowed by Amazon.

So any *writer's club* that arranged for member authors to review each other's books on Amazon, would result in all such reviews being taken off the Amazon site.

Google *RJ Ellory detected, crime writer who faked his own glowing reviews* about an author who manufactured reviews of his own book, using false identities, giving himself 5 star reviews, and slamming competitors in other reviews (known as *sock-puppeting*).

Amazon Book Reviewers:

8   Who are Amazon Book Reviewers?

Let's start with who Amazon Reviewers are.

As mention above, Amazon has a list of <u>thousands of unpaid reviewers</u> who do not work for Amazon.

Amazon has a ranking system for its reviewers and special badges for the Top-Thousand Reviewer, Top-Five Hundred Reviewer, Top-Fifty Reviewer, Top-Ten Reviewer and # One Reviewer ranks.

The Amazon review system provides for:

- a five star system for ranking an item;
- a box for customers to click if they found the review helpful;
- the *most helpful* reviews are placed at the top left of the customer reviews list and the *most recent* ones at the top right; and
- an analysis of the number and distribution of the star rankings along with the average star ranking.

Amazon on occasion bumps up the *most helpful* reviews into its *Spotlight* reviews.

9   Vine:

A program called *Vine* was introduced in 2008, and seems to be available only to the Top-Thousand Reviewers: they get free books in advance of their publication date from publishers and other free products to review and keep if they want to. Their reviews are labeled *Customer Review from the Amazon Vine Program*, and the reviewers get a badge called *Vine Voice* and are referred to as *Voices*.

Here is Amazon's description of their Vine system:

"What is Amazon Vine?

Amazon Vine invites the most trusted reviewers on Amazon to post opinions about new and pre-release items to help their fellow customers make informed purchase decisions. Amazon invites customers to become Vine Voices based on their reviewer rank, which is a reflection of the quality and helpfulness of their reviews as judged by other Amazon customers. Amazon provides Vine members with free products that have been submitted to the program by participating vendors. Vine reviews are the independent opinions of the Vine Voices. The vendor cannot influence, modify or edit the reviews. Amazon does not modify or edit Vine reviews, as long as they comply with our posting guidelines. A Vine review is identified with the green stripe Customer review from the Amazon Vine Program.

Why do you have the Amazon Vine program?

The program was created to provide customers with more information including honest and unbiased feedback from some of Amazon's most trusted reviewers.

How can I join the program?

Amazon Vine is an invitation-only program. Vine Voices are selected based on several criteria, but primarily on the helpfulness of their reviews as judged by all other customers and by their demonstrated interest in the types of products that are featured in the program. Customers who consistently write helpful reviews and develop a reputation for expertise in specific product categories are most likely to be invited into the program."

10   Study of Amazon Reviewers:

The most detailed study to date of Amazon Book Reviewers was done in 2011 by Trevor Pinch and Filip Kesler, entitled *How Aunt Emmy Gets Her Free Lunch: A Study of the Top-Thousand Customer Reviewers at Amazon.com*. Google the title and download the report.

As you read the Pinch-Kesler Amazon Reviewer study, ask yourself how the information on this subset of top Amazon reviewers might assist you in framing your query letter to Amazon Reviewers to review your own book.

Here are a few snippet findings from that study:

Reviewer education –

A large percentage of the 166 respondents in the Pinch-Kesler study had post-high school education (92% college with 56% masters and above degrees – there were 22 doctorates. The country of origin of just under 90% was America.

Reviewer Gender –

An unusual finding is that 70% of the respondents were male – even though some 60% plus readers are women.

Reviewers as Authors –

A striking fact is that 39% of the "top Amazon reviewers" are also authors (and 71% of them are men, with 29% being female writers).

Reviewer Ages –

What about age groups? They are older - the respondents were evenly distributed in the range 30 to 70, with a few more in the 52 to 60 bracket; only 5 of the 166 were under 30.

Volumes of Reviews –

What about the volume of reviews? The most highly ranked Amazon Reviewers produce the bulk of the reviews – the number of reviews done falls away sharply after the Top-Ten rank

Number of Monthly Reviews –

How many reviews do they write each month? About half write less than 6 per month (more than one per week), with 12 of the 166 writing more than 20 each month.

The busiest were very busy indeed – the old 80/20 principle applies. The Big 3 churned out about 11% of the total reviews, with the Big 10 of the 166 responsible for 30%. The 20 fastest reviewers in the group clocked in at more than 20 reviews per month.

Items Reviewed –

Just over half (56%) of the respondents reviewed only books; the rest reviewed books and other items.

Kinds of Books Reviewed –

What kinds of books did the sample review? Most reviewed both non-fiction and fiction books, and non-fiction is more popular than fiction. Mysteries and thrillers are the most popular fiction genre, then came science fiction and fantasy, followed by biography and then politics and current affairs.

Did they review every book they read? No – just over one-third (35%) did. The reason? Most said because they don't have the time or did not like the book, or read for pleasure and not review purposes.

Reasons for choices to review –

Why did they choose the books they chose to review? There were many factors. Some had an expertise and so chose those kinds of books. Some went for books they thought were not properly appreciated. Others only if they have a strong opinion about the book. Some choose based on a whim. More recently published books are more likely to be chosen for review than older books.

Why do they review? –

Why do they review items? More than 80% ranked *self expression* and *enjoyment* in their top 3 reasons for reviewing.

TIP: Can you use <u>self-expression</u> as part of your pitch to your Brand Ambassadors when you ask them to convert to reviewers of your books (which, like John Locke, is your ultimate aim for your Target Readers). Brainstorm with your Team how to word your pitch using this reason why Amazon reviewers in the study wanted to do reviews.

Free books for Reviewers –

What kinds of free books do you get as an Amazon Reviewer?

If Amazon promotes you to the Top-Thousand rank, you will start getting Advance Reading Copies (ARCs) from publishers, often up to 6 months before the book is published.

Otherwise you will be offered free copies to review by the authors themselves, or agents or publishers.

Most of the respondents said they *would* review free books offered to them (50 of the 133 said always, 54 said usually). If this holds true for the Top-Thousand Reviewers, and they reply to your query for a review, your chances of actually getting such a review for your book seem to be delightfully high!

11   Amazon Book Reviewers are Important for You:

Amazon is a groundbreaking pioneer in customer reviews, as well as being the largest online retailer, with a highly sophisticated computer system that allows it to monitor and interact with its huge customer base.

Amazon Reviewers are in the front line of the very important *recommendation and media shopping tools* that you need to use in order to migrate your book up from the thin end of the Long Tail towards the Head.

Your Kindle eBook will be ranked in the Kindle's Bestsellers lists partly on the number of reviews you get, and such a ranking catapults many eBooks into much higher sales.

The *Amazon promotion machine* works in Amazon's interest and the interests of its authors – a win-win model.

Their reviewer system is based on the *third party validation and social proof theory* of how people are influenced to buy products. Social proof means that people are more likely to do something if someone else they trust is doing it. A 2010 poll by Euroconsultancy found that 55% of consumers would be more likely to buy a product if it was highly-rated.

Google *how to increase the social proof of your book marketing* for hints on this important strategy; make sure you read the post by Kissmetrics.

Also Google *10 Ways to Instantly Amplify the Social Proof of Your Marketing Pamela Vaughan* for some good hints.

And Google *social proof for authors buildbookbuzz* for the useful article on how authors can use social proof as part of their marketing of their books.

Once your book sales start moving, the Amazon machine steps in to help both you and it, by placing your book higher in its search results and category lists.

Amazon might also choose your book as one of its <u>book recommendations</u> on the website and in emails to customers.

Amazon also understands the power of repeat buys, and wants its book buyers to buy more books (it sells around two-thirds of the books sold to returning customers), so its machine is geared to making such buyers' choices easier through its *recommendation tools* and *mediated shopping tools*.

Google *How To Get Amazon's Top Customer Reviewers To Review Your Book Joanna Penn* for good hints on this topic.

Joanna Penn writes:

"In fact ... Authors who submitted to popular reviewers on Amazon received 25% more reviews than average and earned 32% more revenue for their latest release. Not necessarily a case of cause and effect but a good sign nonetheless."

12   Amazon's Hall of Fame Reviewers:

Amazon has hit the mother lode with its reward system for its vast army of unpaid reviewers. <u>It figured out that these people would work like crazy for one single but highly important thing: recognition.</u>

Call it the reviewer's fame.

Can you and your Team and your Brand Ambassadors do some brainstorming and come up with ways for you to duplicate Amazon's secret?

Google *Amazon Hall of Fame reviewers* and dip into some of the reviews to get a feel for what Amazon's best reviewers do to deserve that position.

Amazon controls who gets promoted (into the Top Thousand Reviewers, up through the other ranks, right up to the very top), and what is considered in deciding on promotions.

But Amazon has also created a wonderful vehicle for the recognition by the Amazon community at large of these reviewers, *through its ranking and badges,* and now through its Hall of Fame, for those Amazon calls its super-star reviewers.

The Hall of Fame recognizes the multi-year accomplishments of those Amazon calls its elite reviewers. Each member receives a permanent badge which will be displayed next to all future reviews they write. If you reach the Top Ten, you are in. Past superstars were inducted in the Hall of Fame.

Note that one blogger wrote that Amazon had over 30 million people who had reviewed a product on their site, and over 10,000 of them are "very active" reviewers.

How to Contact Amazon Reviewers:
13   The Direct Approach:

Google *amazon's top customer reviewers* to see the list of reviewers. Bookmark this site; it is one you will be doing a lot of work on.

Your Goals:

Your goals in your book reviews part of your Small Steps Plan are to decide on which reviewers to approach, to draft your query letter, to do research on each such reviewer, to approach them, and to have a number write reviews of your book. <u>Your success rate might be a small percentage of the reviewers you approach, but each and every one of them is a very valuable block in your promotion of your book.</u>

Small Steps:

Sounds like a mountain?

Remember your *Small Steps and Small Wins* strategy.

Break your analysis and approach to reviewers down into small chunks, spread over time, to make sure you can succeed at this vital task.

Your Genre Reviewers:

Your first job is to find those reviewers who review books of the same genre as yours. Check their badges to see their ranks. Remember, if one of these reviewers does write a review for your book, that review will have next to it the badge, and that badge speaks volumes to all Amazon customers. So select target reviewers from all the levels of reviewers.

Do your homework:

Now you do your homework on each reviewer you have shortlisted, by clicking on their names and reading their profiles. See below for the kind of homework you must do on each and every reviewer you are thinking of contacting.

You are looking for contact information (email address or physical address).

What if there is no address? You Google the reviewer's name and see if you can track down contact information. If not, move on to the next reviewer.

Once you have contact information, keep your query short and sweet, but make it powerful – see below for tips on how to draft compelling query letters to potential reviewers.

Don't forget to dig into the reviewers' own Facebook pages. And also check the Facebook page in groups for the Amazon reviewers collective page, which you can find here (note the https – not just http) – it is not an official Amazon group but does have Amazon reviewers – so bookmark it and dip into it; click on individual reviewers names to go to their own Facebook pages – follow those you like:

https://www.facebook.com/groups/amazonreviewers/

Add as a task in your Small Steps Plan reading a set number of such reviewers Facebook pages to find out more about them, identify those who might be good choices to review your kind of books, and to follow as well as comment on; then select some to ask for reviews.

Google *amazon top reviewers forum books* then bookmark the site and dip into it for items of interest to you and your Team.

14   The Indirect Route:

Always Ask:

Any time a reader comments on your book on your social network (your Author Blog, your Facebook page, via Twitter, or in response to your participation in forums), reply and ask them politely if they would mind posting a review of your book on Amazon. If you can, add a link to your Amazon Author; once there, they can click on your book and then click on add a review. Mention that any review can be short and sweet (why they liked the book, why they think others would like it etc.).

Experiment:

Experiment with different kinds of requests for reviews, and bounce them off your Team and Clan.

Check Hints:

Google *amazon top reviewers forum* and dip into it for hints from reviewers and others on the whole Amazon review program; you might find some hints on how to ask for reviews.

Google *Rebecca Johnson*, one of the top Amazon Reviewers, and buy her eBook on her lifetime as an Amazon reviewer for some good hints on how to contact reviewers and what to say in your query letter.

And check Rebecca Johnson's blog.

Google *5 Top Tips For Approaching Book Reviewers by Amazon Hall of Fame Reviewer guest @JanetBoyer* for the post on what you should and should not do when querying an Amazon Reviewer to review your book. It includes an example of what Janet Boyer thinks is a good query to a reviewer.

If you get a review, ask the reviewer if you can use the review as a blurb on the cover of your book or for your eBook.

15   What a good Book Reviewer should consider:

One suggestion for a good review was one that provided a description of content (enough to whet the appetite but not too much to spoil it for others); an explanation of why you were delighted or disappointed by the book; and some reasons given why buying and reading this book will make the reader's life better.

Some of the reviewers comment on the plot or on typos. Some deduct points for bad formatting (especially of Kindle eBooks) or failure to provide a table of contents for a book that needed one.

One reviewer explained the rating scale used: a 5 star book was one the reviewer loved; 4 stars means she enjoyed it but if was not a 5 star one; 3 stars meant it was entertaining and others might enjoy the book; 2 or 1 stars meant forgeddabout it.

Google *the secret life of an online book reviewer helen coster* for her interesting article in Forbes. Donald Mitchell, who gets about 40 books a day, mostly directly from the authors, charges for his book reviews and donates the proceeds to Habitat, and, writes Helen Coster, tries to write his reviews as if he was talking to someone:

"Mitchell tries to write reviews as if he's talking to someone, and he knows how to please his audience. "In novels, they want to know how much is action versus how much is the thought process," he says. "I have a mental template that I use.""

16   Should you become an Amazon Book Reviewer?

If you have the time, why not take a crack at it?

You might just be helping to develop the Indie Community by adding to the Amazon book reviewers. Study the top reviewers to see how they review books (the size of their reviews, what they comment on, how they say things, whether they have an opinion on the topics etc.).

And becoming a reviewer of books in the same genre as yours could help increase the visibility of your Author Brand and help boost your own book sales.

Reviewing books in your genre can also help improve your writing skills. I suggest that you compile a checklist of items you think make a book in that genre a good one, and fill it in for every book you review. You could then use these checklists for a series of blog posts in your own Author Blog.

To boost your Author Brand, consider posting *video reviews* of books you have reviewed (see Task 19 for videos); just make sure they are good, and don't detract from your Author Brand.

Sign off your reviews like this: Glenn Ashton, author of *The Euros: Notre Dame Point Zero*. Subtle self-promotion.

17 How to Write an Amazon Book Review:

What did the respondents to the *Pinch-Kesler Amazon Reviewer Study* mentioned above think made a review a good review? The massive winners in the list of 7 factors given to them by Pinch-Kesler to rank were:

- accurate and concise description of the contents;
- a personal distinctive style; and
- demonstrating expertise and familiarity with the topic or genre.

The remaining ones were not ranked anywhere as highly: simple vocabulary; comparison to other books or products; a catchy title.

Respondents were asked what other factors in a review were important. Being fair was one. Help people make a decision but don't make it for them. Put the book in the wider genre it fits into – what was its place? Who would read it, the general public or the expert? The reviewer should have an opinion and should state it. Be entertaining. And read the book you are reviewing!

Reviews can be short and sweet; do you like the book and why, would you recommend it to others etc.

Robert Morris, an Amazon Hall of Fame reviewer, has these good suggestions for writing reviews: only review books you find compelling, and would read anyway; don't write summaries of the books; don't impose your own biases; and have fun.

Google *kindleboards master list of book reviewers* and bookmark it; make it a task in your Small Steps Plan to dip into it periodically to find reviewers and hints on how to approach them.

Other Book Reviewers:

18   Who are they?

Indie Book Reviewers are book reviewers who are not linked to Amazon or any other publisher. Many of them are authors who have compiled lists of Indie Reviewers. Many of these reviewers will review books for free.

One way to track down Indie Book Reviewers is to Google *indie book reviewers* and glance at the many entries.

TIP: Select Indie Book Reviewers who will accept eBooks to review, in order to keep your costs down (if your eBook sells for 99 cents, and your printed book for $15 or more, you get a lot more bank for your buck sending out eBook copies than printed ones!)

19   Indie Book Reviewers by Genre:

Some sources list the reviewers alphabetically, others by genre, which narrows the field down when you are searching for names to approach for your book.

20   Indie Book Review Policies:

It is important to check the book review policies of the Indie Book Reviewers, and to comply with them. There's no point sending a romance out to someone who only wants to review science fiction. Their review policies will indicate what they refer, their preferred genres, whether they will or won't review self-published books, how long it might take for them to review your book, whether they will accept eBooks.

Google *RaeLynn Writes rules for book reviewing* for an example of one book Indie Book Reviewer's. Note that she clearly states where she publishes her reviews (Amazon, B&N, Goodreads, Library Thing and Shelfari). You particularly want reviewers who publish on Amazon.

TIPS for Getting Your Book Reviewed:

21   Prepare your Book Review Plan:

It will form part of your Small Steps Plan.

22   What's in your Book Review Plan?

It should contain the many small steps needed to prepare for, ask, respond to and use book reviews from the various types of reviewers.

It should include using all your social media platforms (your Author Blog, your Facebook page, your Twitter account), as well as Forums.

Your Plan should cover at least a 12 month period, broken down into weeks. Trying to get your book reviewed does not stop when you have a dozen or more reviews. You should aim at continuously seeking new reviews of your book.

The better the fit between the target reviewer and your book, the greater your chance is of having it reviewed by him, and the better the review might be.

Don't forget to thank your reviewers, both the good ones and the not-so-good ones (email or via comments in your blog).

23   Your Reviewer Profile Sheet:

The first step in your Review Promotion Plan is to prepare a *Reviewer Profile Sheet* to guide you and others (Team, your Target Readers, and your Writers' Club) in selecting target researchers to do homework on.

The *Reviewer Profile Sheet* contains a list of facts that will narrow down your search.

On it you should put:

 the genre of your book;

the topics discussed in your book;

the localities mentioned (some reviewers might want to review a book that deals with localities they live in or have visited);

the professions or occupations of your characters (is there a match with the target reviewer or with books he has reviewed in the past?);

your written definition of your Author;

your Author and Book Elevator Speech;

your Keywords for your book;

your Amazon Book Description;

your Target Reader Personas (does the target reviewer "fit" these Personas?);

your own qualifications for writing the book;

whether the reviewer has reviewed the books of your competitors;

will the reviewer do an author interview with you;

where does the reviewer publishes her reviews, and any other factors you and your Team might come up with in your brainstorming sessions.

24 Do your Homework before asking for a review:

You use your *Reviewer Profile Sheet* mentioned above to check possible reviewers.

Doing your Homework means reading the submission requirements of the reviewer; reading reviews of that reviewer to get an idea of how they review; and thinking about how your pitch to that reviewer can be personalized.

Monitor the reviewers on Twitter and their Facebook pages, as well as their websites, blog and places they frequent.

You should pay particular attention to any Forums they might use, because you might want to raise your visibility on those Forums popular with your target reviewer(s).

Bookmark interesting sites with indie and other book reviewers in several directories: a general one; one dealing with just your genre; the biggest sites and smaller sites (measured by Google Page Rank or using the Alexa widget for Firefox and Waterfox – see below), and add sites you like to these. It makes it easier for you to find sites to approach later on.

25 How to Prepare for Asking for a Review:

Your approach to the target reviewer is a two-step one.

First, you comply with the submission guidelines and send a query whether the reviewer would like to receive a free copy of your book to review. If your request is compelling, and the answer is Yes, then you send a further package of information, along with your book.

Your first letter or email must Hook the reviewer, and needs a lot of work. Why should she want to review your book? What made you stand out from the herd?

The first step is to do your Homework – see below for hints on how to do that. Your request for a review must be professional (no typos, correct names used, right tone for that reviewer, right genre for that reviewer).

And it must have a Hook in it, to get his or her attention. What kind of Hook depends on your Homework: as you research the reviewer, *always* be on the lookout for anything you come across that might give you a Hook that is unique and compelling.

If you can relate your book's topic, or localities mentioned in the book, or events, or other items, to the target reviewer, this gives you fertile ground for fashioning your Hook, and getting her to read your query more carefully.

If you can make a personal link between the reviewer and your book or yourself, your chances of hooking her interest are much higher.

Add the link to your *Amazon Author Page*, so that they can click on the book and use the Look Inside feature to read your actual writing.

Make your presentation to the reviewer a professional one, and include items that help her to get to know you, your book, your journey as an author, and what others think of your book).

In your package of information, sent to the reviewer if your query letter succeeded, you should include your book; information about your book (consider your Elevator Speech and your book description); information about yourself (make sure it reflects your Author Brand); perhaps some information about your target readers; reviews by others if you have any; a list of Frequently Asked Questions (FAQs); your Hook based on your Homework; your contact information; and links to your Author Blog and your Amazon Central Author page.

Ask if your target reviewer might wish to publish on her site other information pieces (such as a post for her blog) and whether you could provide them to her.

Foogle Paula Krapf 7 simple steps to a review for hints; she has links to a few review sites.

If a reviewer interviews you, tweet the interview along with a thank you to the reviewer.

26 Sample Book Review Request:

Google *How to Write a Letter to Get a Book Reviewed Carl Hose* for some hints on the contents of your query letter.

Google *Shoot For the Stars: How to Get Testimonials for Your Book Joel Friedlander* for his good list of what you should include in your review request letter.

Note his recommendation that your query letter includes a statement why your book is important (what you wish to achieve with it); this is a good example of weaving a story into your request.

27 Use different requests when asking for a review:

Add as a task to your book review part of your Small Steps Plan experiments with different types of review request letters, after brainstorming with your Team. Keep track of the results so that you can use the most effective ones.

Change the content, the length, the pitch, the tone, the words used, different Elevator Speeches, different 'stories', different book descriptions and keywords etc. until you end up with something that seems to work best for you.

Instead of asking for a 'review' why not ask for a 'blurb' or a 'write up' – sounds a bit less intimidating to some people.

Ask your Target Readers and Writers' Club for examples of good or bad review request letters they have come across.

28   Get the OK to use a Review in your Promotion:

Always get the OK to use any review in your book promotion; most reviewers will say Yes (they benefit from the exposure).

Once you have a few book reviews, get more mileage from them by adding a Label to your Author Blog named *My Book Reviews*, and add that as a label to each post you make which includes a review you have received. Every year, write a post with the best reviews and your comments on them.

29   Target those reviewing your Competitors' Books;

Make a list of reviewers who reviewed their books in your *My Bloggy Book*.

30   Ask Other Writers who might be a good reviewer for you:

Writers are a good source of leads. If you have formed a mutual-help group of Indie authors (your Writers' Club), ask them to suggest reviewers who might be a good fit for your book. If they know the reviewers and are willing, use their name in your query (Starting your query with: Writer X suggested I approach you because [give a reason or two] makes it more personal and just might tip the scales when the reviewer is considering your request.) It's another example of social proof in operation.

31 Check the Blog Reviewer's Google Page Rank:

How do you know if any book reviewer has many readers? Go to the website or blog of the book reviewer, and check the page rank using Google Page Rank.

Or you could install the Alexa toolbar which allows you to check the rankings of any reviewer site from your Firefox or Waterfox browser, when you go to that site. The Alexa ranking appears on the bottom of your screen.

Remember: you are not just targeting those reviewers who are the heavy hitters; you are also targeting mini-markets by asking for reviews from reviewers with smaller audiences.

32 Some Book Reviewer Links:

Google *self-published book reviewer lists* for new lists of reviewers.

TIP: Add as a task in your Small Steps Plan frequent checks for new or revised lists of self-published book reviewers.

Here are some links for you to consider.

Consider joining *Book Blogs*; they sometimes have postings by authors seeking help to get reviews, and other authors respond with lists:

Ask for lists of possible reviewers on the various *Forums* you will be commenting on.

Google *Book Review Blogs That Accept Self-Published Work Karen Woodward*; hat tip to Karen for two lists of indie book reviewing blogs.

The *Fyrefly's Book Blog* has listings of just under 2,000 book review sites, but because they are not grouped together, you need to use the search engine on the site to find ones you might wish to check. Here's how to get to fyreflybooks' search engine (which uses Google's Custom Search so that your search locates book bloggers):

https://fyreflybooks.wordpress.com/about/book-blogs-search/

Read the comments in *fyreflybooks* for listings by others of their favorite book bloggers.

You use it by typing in these keywords: book review, review blogs, book blog, or book bloggers.

For more hints and links to indie book review sites, buy a copy of my eBook *Your Purrfect Way to Publishing & Promoting Your Amazon & Kindle Book* for 99 cents from my Amazon author site at

https://www.amazon.com/author/glennashton

1   Amazon's Meet Our Authors Forum:

TIP: *Choosing Forums* - Remember Rebecca Random when choosing the Forums sandboxes you want to play in; let the gods of chance play a role in your selection by choosing at least 20% of your target Forums by random. You just might find a lot of Rebecca Randoms playing in those sandboxes!

TIP: *Finding Forums* – Google *forums* and your genre or theme to find forums.

Google *amazon meet our authors forum* for access to the forum created by Amazon in May 2011 for Indie publishers like you, with over 1,000 discussions. There is a search box you can use. On the bottom of the page is a listing of the most active community forums on Amazon, which includes Meet our Authors.

Authors exchange advice about writing, and about promoting their books, on this forum. Some readers do dip into the posts to find new readers, but it is largely author conversations with author. Some threads deal only with one genre, while others deal only with book promotion.

Say hello on a few of the threads that suit your genre or the stage of your Indie journey. Visit the blogs of other authors on those threads, to see how they are promoting their Author Blogs and their books.

Jot down interesting ideas on book promotion in *My Bloggy Book*, for later use.

TIP: See if you can find authors interested in joining your very own **Writers Club**.

Remember *Headlines that Hook*? The name of the thread is all other authors see, so make your posts stand out, interesting and intriguing. You narrow the field down by adding your genre in your introduction of yourself. Brainstorm some interesting thread titles with your Team, to make them clickable. Think of your themes, your keywords, your Elevator Speech, and your Author Brand when brainstorming: what can make your headlines stand out?

Self-promotion is allowed by Amazon in MOA. So read how others have gone about it, ponder and learn, and then create unique, interesting ways to promote your Author Brand, your Indie journey and your books. Links are allowed.

Rise above the herd.

One author describes posting your own book on MOA is like sticking your business card up on the Great Wall of China, it gets lost so easily.

What can you offer that is of value to other authors?

- A quiz of your Target Readers about some aspect of promoting Indie books?
- Some nugget of advice on useful links to posts by others on other sites about the art of writing and publishing?
- Your own Small Steps Plan and how it might help other authors just starting out on the same Indie journey?
- Invitations for other authors to join your Clan in return for your doing the same for them?

- Descriptions of what your Brand Ambassadors are expected to do and invitations to other writers to join you as an ambassador and you will join them as one of theirs?

Google *galleycat free sites to promote your eBook* for more than 20 such sites. Add some of the sites to your Forum Plan.

Also Google *Jade Kerrion free promotions* for a list of sites on which to publish your book when it is going to be free on Amazon or Kindle.

2   Amazon's & Kindle's Discussion & Book Forums

See Task 7 above.

Google *amazon forum book* for a listing of threads discussing books.

Google *kindle the book corner* for a listing of threads discussing books there.

If you download free self-published Amazon and Kindle books, consider posting discussions of these books on these two forums, so as to promote the Indie Community.

3   Indie Book Collective:

You can join this if you are "putting the elbow-grease into marketing" your own book, even if you are a rank beginner. It is a collective of Indie publishers, like you.

It aims at helping authors get their books in front of readers

4   Book Clubs and You:

Why is this important? Because <u>more than 5 million Americans belong to book clubs!</u> One commentator describes book clubs as the "invisible army for consumer book of the mouth".

TIP: Your Forum plan portion of your Small Steps Plan should include some tasks dealing with how to find, select and work with book clubs, even if they are only those in your neighborhood.

Think Google+ Hangouts if you cannot travel to the book clubs (see Task 8).

Google *Infinity books book club members like self-published books* for an article by Sherrie Wilkolaski on a few places where you can negotiate having book clubs feature your Indie books (including meetup.com, book-club-queen.com, book-clubs-resource.com).

She also suggests making your own Author Blog book club friendly by setting up a book club welcome page for book clubbers to enjoy (add your Elevator Speech and a few reasons why your book is a good fit for a book club). Include a list of Top 10 discussion questions for book clubs to download or print from your Author Blog, for use when discussing your book.

Can you think of rewards of value you can offer book clubbers for joining your email list?

Can you offer to talk to book clubs by email, telephone, or Skype, about your book?

5   Gaiaonline

Google *gaiaonline* for the Wikipedia article on this forum. It gets a million posts a day, and is visited by more than 7 million daily, of the 23 million registered users. It specializes in games, but its forums are public message boards, many dealing with the games, but others more general. It is the world's biggest hangout for teens and young adults. How can you use it? Check out the gaiaonline writing arena discussion area, and the artists corner.

6   Big Board List of Forums

It tracks the most active forums and boards and has over 2,000 boards in its database. Flip through its rankings. The number of posts and members is shown in the right hand columns next to each forum.

7   JLA Forums

A total of over 207 million posts with more than 3 million attachments in its Forums.

8   Somethingawful Forums

Over 174,000 registered users with over 3 million direct threads and more than 138 million posts. Check out The Book Barn. Costs under $10 to join (to weed out spammers) and users call themselves Goons.

9   Christianforums

More than 62 million posts in 7 million threads and with 325,000 members. Check Wriers Guild under Hobbies, a forum for discussions about how to get published. A place for your Indie journey reflections? Any ethical dilemmas in your book that might find a hearing here?

Has a wide variety of thread groupings you should dip into (life stages, entertainment, hobbies, society, religions, ethics, business, history, news, politics, life sciences, military, regions, recovery, outdoors and nature, recipes etc.

10   Webrat's Forum Book Forum

The book forum of Webrats has discussions of novels, authors and eBooks.

Webrats has over 2,000 active members, one million threads and 2.5 million posts.

11   Abovetopsecret.com science fiction forum

Covers UFOs and conspiracies; some posts have over 30,000 threads.

12   Forums.Catholic.com

All things Catholic at the largest Catholic Community on the Web, with over 300,000 members. Open to non-Catholics. The Water Cooler allows discussions about topics not provided for elsewhere on the site.

13   Essentialbaby Forum

Australian forum dealing with family and kid matters, up to teenagers, with 14 million posts from 235,000 members.

14   TheTrekBBS science fiction forum

Science fiction forum with 123,000 threads in 4.6 million posts and 22,000 plus members.

15   James Randi Educational Foundation Forum

Religion, conspiracy, paranormal and science topics in this forum, with 197,000 threads, 9 million posts, 31,000 members and over 2,000 active members.

16   Skeptic.org Forum

Total posts over 1,200 and topics 200 plus with 170 plus members.

17   Ourlittleuniverse Forum

Community of people with opinions on many subjects, and debates. More than 154,000 threads in 9.5 million posts and with just under 13,000 members.

18   Absolutewrite Forums

Gathering place for members from around the world, this site has a General Writing Interest section worth visiting.

With 218,000 threads in 7.6 million posts and more than 50,000 members, the forum has several genre threads.

Has a blog review section worth exploring. The Writing Lab is the spot to visit if you need some advice on plot endings etc.

19   Syfy Forum

Discussion forum for fiction, with conversations about stories and books with science fiction themes. With 6.6 million posts and 157,000 members.

20   Deviantart Forum for general discussions

General based discussions, with a Literature section, and a Books review one.

21   Unexplained-Mysteries Forum Writers and Artists Hangout

With 4.6 million posts and over 111,000 members, the forum has conversations about science fiction, science and the paranormal.

22   SciForums

Science and science fiction forum with just under 20,000 members, 100,000 plus threads and 2.9 million posts.

23   Theology.com Forums

Politics, religion and general talks with over 44,000 threads in 1.7 million posts and more than 14,000 members.

24   Ntwriters proboards form

Writer hangout. Some 2.4 million posts on over 44,000 topics with 2,300 plus members.

25   Bad Astronomy and Universe Today Forum

Bautforum is for people with ideas outside the mainstream; 1.9 million posts and over 110,000 members.

26   Slackercentral.com board

With 1.5 million posts from just under 7,000 members, the Off Topic section covers anything.

27   Lets Yada Yada Yada Forum

All about parenting and pregnancy, kids including teenagers; 1.5 million posts from around 7,000 members.

28   Thebabycorner.com boards

Has menu with local forums. Kids and parenting.

29   Hostboard.com forum

Has a Books category in the Arts section. Has 180,000 threads in 1.8 million posts with over 201,000 members. Check out the Book Lovers Corner.

30   Magicmum.com

All about motherhood and children; 5.3 million posts with just under 500,000 threads and more than 32,000 members. Has a Magicmum book club section.

31   Wordforge Forum

Conversations about philosophy, politics, religion and combinations in The Red Room; hunting, fishing and outdoors; 1.1 million posts and just under 8,000 members.

32   Sffchronicles Book Writing Forum

Science fiction and fantasy forum, with a book club. Total members just under 35,000 and more than 1.6 million posts and 63,000 threads.

33   Top Forums toplist

Hosts just under 3,000 lists with a total of more than 507,000 sites. Browse to find something that fits your book or your Indie journey.

34   Hypernet ufo forums & blogs

For the science fiction and UFO fans, a listing of sites.

35   Amazon.com Forum Science Fiction

Over 1,000 discussions on this Amazon Science Fiction forum.

36   Ereader IQ listings

Listing of free and discounted eBooks on Amazon and Kindle.

1   Introduction:

In Task 4 above you set about forming your very important Team, who are your essential sounding board and passengers on your Indie journey. Now it is time to take the step of forming a similar group of advisors, only this one has members from your Clan.

2   What they can do for you

Brainstorm with your local Team what they think your Clan Dream Team might be best able to help you with; and also test the contents of your proposals to the Clan Dream Team with your local team first, before sending them out.

To do so, you ask your email subscribers in your follow up email messages whether they might be interested in helping you on your journey as an Indie author, by joining your Online Team.

You give a short description of what your two Dream Teams will be doing.

3   Skill sets of Clan members

You could also ask your subscribers to indicate what range of skill sets they might bring to your online Clan Dream Team of advisors, by giving a menu of skill sets you are looking for, and asking them to check all the boxes they feel they qualify for.

Your menu of skill sets would include a general category, so that you don't scare off people who would make a good member of your Clan Dream Team just because they don't have the narrow skill sets you are looking for.

Add a category such as *Interested in helping the Indie Community to develop*, for example. It must be wide enough that it fits keeners.

4 The search for Connectors
You are looking for what Malcolm Gladwell calls **Connectors** (socially plugged in influencers), with a dollop of **Mavens** (experts, knowledgeable) thrown in.

5 Briefing notes to potential Clan members
You send to all those who respond that they are interested, the same materials explaining what the Dream Team does, that you use with your local Dream.

Point out that membership in your Dream Teams automatically means membership in your Clan of followers, and that any Clan Dream Team member will be expected to become your Brand Ambassador, and will be recognized as such.

Sketch out what kinds of tasks Clan Dream Team advisors will be expected to carry out – this list will be shorter than those your local Dream Team will perform because you cannot expect your online advisors to be as enthusiastic as your handpicked local Dream Team members will be.

You can then decide who should join your Clan Dream Team of advisors (start with the principle that all those who indicated they were interested will be invited to join, and reject only those you really feel would hinder or harm you). You cannot lose if you have dozens of advisors that want to help you decide on topics for future blog posts, or on competitions to engage your readers, or on forums you should consider participating in etc..

Give them a menu of tasks they can help you with, and let them choose which ones they want to participate in.

6   Quid Pro Quo for your Clan Team:

Because they have volunteered to help you, and to not only join your Clan of followers but to sign up for your email subscriber list and receive your Newsletter, and to become your Brand Ambassador, you should offer to return the favor.

If anyone joins, offer to become a member of their own Clan Dream Team should they decide to become a Rebel and publish on Amazon and Kindle, and need advisors. Put a drop dead date on your offer (say, 24 months) so that you are not committing to an open-ended job.

7   Levels of Interaction with Advisors:

You will probably end up with 3 distinct sets of interaction with 3 distinct groups of people who have agreed to advise you on your Indie journey.

The most intensive interaction will be of a one-on-one type with your local *Team*. Given your ability to talk to them, and your selection of them from people you know and who know you, you will have a deeper relationship with them to start off with; the work you do together will be the really heavy lifting in your Promotion Plan.

Next in degree of interaction will be your relationship with members of your online *Clan Dream Team* of advisors. They will perform tasks that help you as an Indie author, but that are less frequent than, and less intensive than, those tasks your local Dream Team perform. This does not mean their input will be inferior, or less worthy.

Far from it: by definition, they are selected from your readers, and their views and help will reflect that.

Finally, your lowest interaction (in an advisory sense) will be with other readers who have joined your email subscribers lists, and who have volunteered in response to your periodic requests for help, to assist you with defined tasks. This will be on an intermittent basis, and mostly task-specific. You will use your requests for such specific assistance as a means to increase the engagement of your readers with you.

This authors' site is relatively new and smallish, with less than a thousand members right now. If you are a published or self-published author, and have a book listed on Amazon, Barnes and Noble, Kindle, etc., you are eligible for joining it.

Entry fee is a modest $5, to keep spammers at bay.

The site offers you a platform to promote your books, to connect with readers and with writers.

You establish your lifetime Author Profile, and can list all your printed or electronic books.

It has a social network platform, and allows you to create your own groups and forums.

Dip into the site and join it.

TIP: Use YourBookAuthors as your Ideas Incubation Laboratory

Add as a task in your Small Steps Plan joining this site, and brainstorm with your Team how you use it to sharpen your various promotions.

Your Guinea Pig Group:

I recommend that you consider YourBookAuthors as your incubation laboratory, where you can design, launch and test many of your promotion actions flowing from your Small Steps Plan.

Because it is relatively small, it gives you a chance to meet electronically with many authors, and to draw upon their experience and expertise to test your ideas.

Consider using authors on the site as your guinea pigs for testing ideas. Offer to reciprocate, and to share with them your best practices, if they will agree to help you.

Invite them to join your **Guinea Pig Group** which will allow you to test some of your promotion ideas before launching them on a wide scale.

Among the things you should brainstorm with your Team to use in your Guinea Pig Group are:

1. Testing how to design, implement and refine **author interviews**, which will all require reciprocal interviews by authors participating (with publication on the participants' author blogs);

2. Testing any **quizzes** you and your Team design to gather more demographic information from your readers, so as to make your messages more precise;

3. Asking for **feedback** on the content of some of your messages, using your specially designed feedback checklists;

4. Advice on your **Target Readers Personas**;

5. Designing **cooperative promotional activities** (see Task 19);

6. Using them as **sounding boards** to give you and your Team more input on your many small steps that your Small Steps Plan will be spinning off once you gain traction;

7. Offer them a free copy of my book, *Small Steps to Bigger Book Sales*, if they will consider **becoming part of your promotional actions**, in return for you offering to do the same

for them (without anyone having to breach any rules of Amazon, Kindle or other forums).

The benefit you offer them will be (a) to share your best practices with them, and (b) reciprocity if they launch their own Guinea Pig Group with YourBookAuthors members.

In a sense, all cooperative efforts among the authors willing to work with you to develop better promotional ideas, will amount to participating authors agreeing to become each other's guinea pigs, in a supportive environment.

1   What is LinkedIn?

At first a place for virtual resumes, it is now a virtual meeting place for professionals. The main aim is to help its members find jobs.

You can join the groups, and add your Twitter and blog feed to your LinkedIn page.

With more than 200 million members, LinkedIn is designed to keep members informed about their industries, find people they need in their business lives, and to exert some control over their professional online identity.

LinkedIn is the world's largest professional virtual network and is in over 200 countries; available in 19 languages; with 200 million members of which 74 million are in the USA, 7 million in Canada, and over 20 million students and recent college graduates.

2   How do You join LinkedIn?

To join, you sign up at the LinkedIn site, and create your profile.

3   What do you do once you've joined LinkedIn?

How do you use it? You search for authors, agents and publishers, and connect with them in Groups.

Google *mashable linkedin beginners guide* for some handy tips on how to go about joining and participating in LinkedIn.

You can seek help with your writing. Or you can seek testimonials from LinkedIn writers – blurbs for your book cover.

If you want to interview other authors, try finding them on LinkedIn.

Google *linkedin authors* for articles on ways to use LinkedIn as a writer.

The key is to become a Joiner.

Join Groups.

Join the conversations.

Don't sit and wait for the lightning to strike. Don't self-promote, but comment, ask questions, join the discussions.

Google *brilliant bloggers talk about linkedin* for some very helpful articles on using LinkedIn.

Google *24 ways to promote your book on linkedin* for some pretty neat hints by Viveka VonRosen on how an author can promote on LinkedIn.

These include:

1. Using Amazon's *Reading List* on LinkedIn by commenting on your book there;
2. asking friends to list your book on Amazon's *Reading List*;
3. add your book to your Professional Headline section (120 characters);
4. add your book to your Experience section;
5. linking to your Amazon Author Central page by Editing your website to read *Buy my book here* with a direct URL to that site;
6. add an extract of your book in your *Contact Me* section.

4   What is LinkedIn etiquette?

Google *q&a linkedin etiquette* for a one page PDF on how to behave on LinkedIn.

5   Your LinkedIn Profile

Your profile is important. You should link your book site to it (your Amazon Author Central page), and your Author Videos, your Book Videos, your Author Blog, your Twitter address, and your Facebook page.

Google *You Can Now Easily Add Media to Your LinkedIn Profile* for instructions on how to easily add pictures, your Author and Book Videos, images, documents, presentations, and your Author Blog posts, etc. with a simple click.

6   How to make connections on LinkedIn

You have a list of Connections on LinkedIn, who are people with whom you have some kind of link: you invite people to join you as a Connection, even if they are not a member of LinkedIn, but if they refuse (they can say I don't know, or worse still, label you as Spam), this is a black mark against you. Too many black marks could lead to you being turfed out of LinkedIn, to discourage shot gunning enrolment campaigns.

7   How do you use your Connections?

You have 3 kinds of connections: your first level of direct connections; then the connections of those people, called second-degree connections; and finally the connections of that second level connections, called third-degree connections.

You use your Connections to find a job, or some business opportunity, or an introduction to someone you don't know but your connection knows. Businesses use LinkedIn to find employees. If any of your connections knows the manager of a business looking to fill a job (as shown by their profiles), you might be able to get a direct introduction to that manager. You can even follow specific companies to see what jobs they are trying to fill using LinkedIn. To help you in your job search, you can bookmark jobs you want to follow up on.

8   Use LinkedIn Answers if you have any Questions

Use LinkedIn Answers to seek help with something to do with your promotion or writing. You pose a question and other LinkedInners can decide to help you, or find someone equipped to help you. Make sure your question is a thoughtful one, that clearly says to people that you have done your homework, and know the type of help you need help with.

Do you want to be a guest on a video show? Ask.

Do you want to set up a Google+ Circle or Hangout with people of defined skillsets, to talk about some specific problems or opportunities? Ask.

And you shall receive. Probably. If you did your homework, and helping you helps the other person as well.

When you use the free service LinkedIn Questions, you cast your query onto the community waters, and those who wish to, will Answer.

Bear in mind that most LinkedIn members are professionals in business or professions.

9   Joining LinkedIn Groups

There are 1.2 million Groups on LinkedIn (2013), with memberships ranging from 1 to over 744,000. Most of the Groups are employment related but there are many others. Groups are managed by their owners, and may be open to members only or to everyone. You usually have to join to be able to post messages.

You may join up to 50 Groups, but should consider a handful only if you are going to make serious contributions to the Groups' conversations.

TIP: Add as a task to the Social Network part of your Small Steps Plan, researching LinkedIn Groups with a view to joining a few and adding to your Author Brand's visibility by engaging in value-added conversations on those groups.

Open Groups allow you to join discussions without becoming a member of the Group first.

As a writer, you can join publishing groups, and polish your credentials for speaking or teaching assignments, if you are heading that way.

Google *linkedin groups authors* for sites dealing with Groups of authors and publishers on LinkedIn.

Google *linkededs & writers* for the biggest LinkedIn Group for editors and writers; it has several subgroups; its goal is to be the preferred space on LinkedIn for wordsmiths to share advice, triumphs and frustrations.

Google *the 20 essential linkedin groups for aspiring writers* and check out the various Groups there with a view to joining some.

Google *linkedin groups for eBook authors, publishers and readers* for a list of Groups of interest to eBook authors.

Google *linkedin groups getting started* for some very good information on how groups can be set up and work, from the LinkedIn Help group.

Google *getting started with linkedin groups for teachers* for a very good article by the TeachThought website on the things you need to consider in choosing Groups, and the way to introduce yourself and submit questions etc.

10   *Creating your Own LinkedIn Group* –

You can create your own group focused on a topic of your choosing or an industry. Brainstorm with your Team, and ask your email Newsletter subscribers, for ideas on suitable topics for your to start on LinkedIn. You need a Group that will appeal to many out there. You might want to consider some Groups dealing with the Indie Community.

TIP: Google *5 tips for effectively managing a linkedin group* if you are thinking of starting your own LinkedIn group. Read that article whether you plan to do it alone, or as a collaborative effort with your own Writers Club or Clan of followers or members of the Indie Community you asked to join you.

The post by Stephanie Sammans on Social Media Examiner includes tips on setting your own Group's rules and policy; screening new members and members discussion posts; using the Group Announcements feature; leading your group (by posting weekly discussions and questions, commenting, and encouraging engagement).

11   TIP on using LinkedIn

Google *20 Tips to Becoming Successful on LinkedIn – Refreshed and Expanded* for some hints on how best to use LinkedIn.

You should also dip into the LinkedIn chat Twitter stream at #LinkedInChat.

---

1   What Book Videos can you can make?

You need an Author Video and Book Video Plan as part of your overall Small Steps Plan. And this plan will include the making of an Author Video, featuring you, and an Book Video, featuring your book, as well as a series of later videos.

Book videos are also known as book trailers, and are a powerful force in marketing books. They can serve as an infomercial, or your own tutorials or webinars.

Kingdom Elect Lady has an article *Create Your Own Book Trailer Free* with hints on how to do just that. She uses still photos set to music.

Your Book Video can be acted out, have animations, simple still photos set to music, you reading extracts of your book, and combinations.

Most book videos run for 1 to 3 minutes.

Your Book Video should grab (hook) the viewer and make them want to read the book.

2   What are Podcasts?

Podcast is a combination of iPod and broadcasting. A podcast is an audio file, hosted on the Web, that is always available to listeners. You can recycle any audio recordings you have (those interviews with your Team, or selected Brand Ambassadors, or someone acting as one of the characters in your book, or with someone interviewing you, the author) into a podcast and make it available to your Target Readers and others.

Podcasts can be downloaded onto personal computers or iPods.

Check out podcasts to get ideas for what might work for your own Author Brand, your book and your goals in your Promotion Plan.

Google *iTunes meet the author* for free author podcasts (you can download iTunes to your computer if you wish).

Also Google *where to find free author podcasts* for other sites.

Google *weekend reading 21 brilliant bloggers talk about starting a podcast* for some very good hints on how to do that.

Google *The Ultimate Guide to Becoming a Podcaster eBook* for a 161 free download eBook by Daniel M. Clark. It covers choosing a topic, equipment, recording and editing, uploading and promoting. Save it and open with Adobe.

Google *Learn How To Podcast 101 podcast answer man* for a video tutorial (120 minutes) that gives you all the building blocks to launch your podcast properly, including using 100% free online services.

Read Irene Watson's article in *chapterandverse* headed *How to Make a Book Video Trailer chapter and verse*. She recommends that you:

1. Think like a screenwriter when you write the words in the script, thinking of the images behind the words and the images you will use.
2. Make it snappy, move those images along, but keep text on the screen long enough for people to read it.
3. Add some of *You* into the mix because people are curious about what makes writers tick.
4. Flash words to segue into the next part.

5. Don't use music with words because they might draw attention away from your own message.

3 Why use book and author videos?

These videos are part of your promotion Plan, designed to impress your Author Brand upon those listening or watching them, and to meet your 3 primary goals.

Consider a series of book videos, dealing with your Indie Journey (introducing yourself as author, your book, your book's characters, your own Writers Club, your overall Promotion Plan, your Team, some of your Brand Ambassadors, your Target Readers reading from your book etc.).

If you embed your video into your Author Page then because YouTube or Google video are the video hosts, they bear the bandwidth hit when someone views your video.

Google *findmeanauthor book trailer videos* for an article on how the videos can help you.

Your Book Video acts like a movie trailer, to entice buyers to read the book. It should increase traffic to your Author Blog.

Other ways to use video as an author (hat tip to Joanna Penn of bookmarketingmaven):

- A video greeting to your Author Page, to personalize it and you;
- One promoting yourself as an author;
- A book video (graphics, words, music);
- Vlog it (make video posts to your Author Blog);
- Video testimonials by your Brand Ambassadors;
- Interviews of you;

- Only 30 to 90 seconds;
- Include your Author Blog address in all videos and a call to action;
- Promote your videos in your Newsletters.

And you can crowdsource your book videos by asking your Target Readers to send in their free versions of book videos of your book, with prizes for those you select to run as part of your Target Reader Book Video Contest.

4   Summary: How to Make your Book Video

Follow the steps outlined by Michelle Pillow in *How to Make Book Videos: The Basics.*

She walks you through her tutorial, using the free Microsoft Movie Maker program. She says using that program is as easy as drag and drop. The Microsoft website has a detailed listing on how to use Movie Maker.

She also has a few author and book videos for you to watch to get an idea of how some people handle it. Searching YouTube for book trailers is another way to see what's out there. She recommends no more than 2 minutes for a book trailer.

Google *brenda coulter promoting your novel how to make a book trailer* for her description of her experience in making her own book video.

If YouTube videos only have a shelf life of about 3 to 6 weeks, then you should consider a series of videos.

Google *ivanhoejenny how to make book trailers* for Jenny Butler's very good checklist of steps to take, and links to some good free sources you can use.

Among her very practical and useful points are these:

1. Put 5 points of the most important things you want to say about your book into your brand new Video Folder as your Plot;
2. Think what best gets these ideas across (think text, images, music) and jot them down for your Video Folder;
3. Collect your images;
4. Collect your background music;
5. Collect your sound effects;
6. Put it all together and use the acid test: will this make people buy your book?
7. Don't forget to include your book cover.

Read Claudia Jackson's *How to Make a Book Trailer* for some good pointers. She used Twitter to get views of her first book trailer from her "tweeple", then she uploaded it to YouTube. Her pencil scribbles morphed into her storyboard and onto paper. She used a scene list and well as her script. Spend time on thinking how to tease viewers. Her book trailers usually take her between 50 and 100 hours to make. She also includes a list of 23 sites you can upload your book video to.

Consider joining *Book Trailer Central Community*. It connects readers and authors through book trailers.

You should read *squidoo book trailers* for articles on how to, where to, and why regarding book videos. One author comments that book videos are part of her establishing her Author Brand by connecting with the public; by watching the video they will get an impression of her as author.

Also Google *rachelle gardner how to make your own book trailer* for some very practical and simple how to instructions on going about your own book video. Windows Live Movie Maker is used, and the advice in the article is always use a tripod when taking photographs. Use music from a royalty free site (named in the article). The writer uploaded the video to YouTube and then embedded it in her website, and added it to her author profiles on Goodreads, shared it through her blog posts. To use the video on Amazon, a YouTube upload will not work; a direct file is needed.

Another very interesting site is *booktrailersforreaders*, especially the article on *How to Make a Book Trailer* by Michelle Harclerode. Micelle uses Photo Story as the program.

And finally check out *Book Video Trailers: 11 Steps to Make Your Own* by Joanna Penn. Joanna used Windows Movie Maker to produce the video in the article (photos plus text plus music; no moving images).

5   Using Vlogs (Video Blogs) as Webinars

Your Vlogs can be longer than the book videos (up to 10 minutes if the subject matter is meaty.

Make sure that *You* come through loudly and clearly, and that the Vlog fits your Author Brand.

Brainstorm the script, the players, the settings with your Team.

Storyboard your ideas first.

Make sure there are plenty of Hooks in it, plus Calls to Action.

6   Free Programs to Make your Video

Check *Photo Story* by Microsoft (free) and Microsoft *Movie Maker* (also free).

As a self-published author (on Amazon or Kindle or some other printing base), you are a Rebel.

The target of your rebellion is the conventional printing industry. By keeping control of the conventional printing presses, these outdated barons have managed to set back the spread of the printed word by imposing their own funnel on it. Because they cannot print everything authors want to print, they have been able to force their wishes and wants on to the industry.

But those days are over now.

Independent self-publishers are ushering in the Indie Revolution in every greater numbers. However, as a new industry, it needs support to ensure its viability.

And that is where we come in.

It is in our interests to cooperate with other self-publishing Indies in order to sustain the Revolution, and improve the quality of its product, and its distribution. That is why I wrote this book.

TIP: Add as a task to your Small Steps Plan brainstorming sessions with your local and online Teams of advisors, to come up with ideas of how to improve the self-publishing industry.

For starters, carefully read through this book and check all ideas that might usefully be employed to boost the chances of success of Indie authors. If you like an idea, ask yourself why it cannot be used in a cooperative effort with other authors to do just that.

It's clear that many self-published authors need help in two main areas: the quality of their books, and in selling their books. Yet within the Indie industry are tens of thousands of intelligent, well-meaning people (like you), who have the ability to offer highly professional help to such authors, in both fields.

In unity is strength.

Doing everything on your own is draining; that is why so many management and life experts recommend working with Mastermind or guidance experts. And that is why Small Steps to Bigger Book Sales is founded on using, from the get-go, your own Team, and later on extending it to an internet-based team as well.

The Indie Bottlenecks:

There are a handful of bottlenecks in the self-publishing industry which Indie authors as a whole could easily reduce.

The major pinch points are:
1. Improving the quality of book writing;
2. Acting as a sounding board to improve the production of books (layout etc.);
3. Helping to prepare effective, manageable promotion plans for Indie authors;
4. Participating in the carrying out of such promotion plans through advice – the guinea pig concept.

The Colorado Independent Publishers Association is an example of a formal corporate body doing just this. So does the Alliance for Independent Authors on their blog.

Also, google *Why Self-Publishers Should Go it Alone, Together Joel Friedlander* for a discussion of writers' cooperatives aimed at working together to help each other.

This is the plea by *J. Glenn Evans* in his blog post at The Independent Publisher:

"Authors who self-publish or use PODs should organize to support each other with newsletters and websites that would include book reviews and notices of new releases. This would generate interest and support for books of merit. Among its goals should be providing greater exposure for member's books. Self-written or commissioned reviews should be permitted, but first screened by individuals qualified to judge their merit. This would be the qualification for publication through the association's newsletters and website. Reviewers and booksellers who give author/self-publishers and author/PODs a fair shake should be listed and supported by members of the association. They could provide networking support and patronage while encouraging their friends and other contacts to do the same."

If you want to keep track of one man's efforts to further this POD revolution, then <u>email Glenn Evans</u> and tell him to copy you on progress from his viewpoint.

Who knows? You might be on the cutting edge of a leap forward in cooperative Indie publishing! His email is info@poetswest.com – he asked people to contact him.

The *independent cooperative Peoples-Ink* have just launched their first cooperative effort- email them to keep in touch with their efforts for a tightly-focused group doing a lot together:

"We envision a writer's community where members can start and develop a written piece through our workshops and discussion groups, then publish and promote their finished writing with cooperative releases, all absolutely free. It's a new, community oriented way of writing and publishing for Portland and beyond.

Future releases are planned. If you have a book you that you'd eventually like to put out into the world, contact us at info@peoples-ink.com. We can help."

Google *writers cooperatives* for more articles and groups.

TIPS for Your Indie cooperative efforts:

Here are a few ideas for you to talk to your Team about and then to other writers:

1. Offer moral support to other self-published authors (email them, subscribe to their email services, comment on their Facebook pages, blogs and other channels, offer to talk through DM about shared issues etc.).
2. Offer to join their Brand Ambassador group – perhaps on a reciprocal basis?
3. Offer to beta-read a chapter of their future book(s).
4. Establish a Google+ Hangout and Circle dedicated to cooperative efforts of self-published authors, and spread news of its existence through your own distribution channels; encourage other writers to join them.

5. Consider joint promotions of future or current books, in selected channels.
6. Offer membership to co-authors in your internet Clan of followers, on a reciprocal basis.
7. Work with other authors to form an internet based talent and skills exchange – a data bank would display ranges of talents of members, and talents would be offered on a no-fee, no-liability, reciprocity base.
8. Start your own Indie Newsletter, and ask other authors to add your signup form to their messages to their email subscribers, and also to submit articles for the newsletter. Encourage other newsletters, with parts open for cross-published posts on the concept of self-publishing cooperation.

Add as a task to your Small Steps Plan periodic reviews with your Team of your whole promotion effort.

Take each element of your Small Steps Plan in turn, and go over what your Plan said you would do, what you did, what the results were, and what worked or did not work.

Re-think the Plan.

If it took too much time (your time and that of your Team), then scale it back. If its goals were too vague, then tighten them up. Remember John Locke's original goals he set himself: few in number, but ones he could meet. Then he moved the goalposts.

Consider adding more detail to your Editorial Contents Report: a more detailed spreadsheet, setting out the various parts of your Small Steps Plan, and covering a longer period, with more small chunks of work included.

Ask your Clan if some of them would like to provide input into the Plan and its success. If they do, provide a results summary, and ask them to give you feedback on specific points.

Pay especial attention to your Target Readers Personas. Massage them, add some new ones, play a bit more with Rebecca Random.

Tighten them up: remember John Locke's sound advice, to look the narrowest possible niches in the market and aim relentlessly at them.

SMALL STEPS PLAN

Period covered: From　　　　to　　　　　.
Key:
Enter the target date for doing the task in one of the six monthly columns on the right. The number refers to the paragraph in that Task chapter (so 1.3 refers to subparagraph 3 of Task 1 chapter).

Task:	Describe Task							
Task 1:	**Dream Team of Advisors:**							
1.3	Decide on people to invite to join my local Dream Team							
	Prepare Dream Team mandate							
1.5	Give copies of the *Small Steps to Bigger Book Sales* to potential members of my Team							
1.8	Ask Team to invite their relatives and friends to join my Clan so as to kick start it							
	Invite people to join my Team							
1.4	Decide on when and how the Team will meet							

Task:	Describe Task							
1.7	Prepare first draft of Editorial Contents Plan for brainstorming with Team							
Task 2:	**My Author Plan:**							
2.3	Brief review of Author Brands of my genre-competitors							
2.3, 2.4	Write down definitions of possible Author Brands for use with my Team							
2.3	Brainstorm possible definitions with my Team							
2.4	Use Mind Mapping with my Team about my Author Brand							
2.6	Prepare my Author Branding Story							
2.8	Prepare my Author Brand Elevator Speech							
2.8	Test the Author Brand Elevator Speech with my Team, friends and others							
2.3, 2.10	Check all the brand elements with my Team							
2.8	Draft my Book Elevator Speech							

Task:	Describe Task								
2.8	Test my Book Elevator Speech with my Team								
Task 3:	**My Target Readers:**								
3.2, 3.9, 3.14	Develop the Target Reader Personas (including Rebecca Random)								
3.14, 3.18	Brainstorm the Personas with my Team								
3.12, 3.20	Ask my Target Readers to help define Personas (at a later stage)								
3.21	Prepare Surveys of my Target Readers about their demographics, for use in testing and revising my Personas								
3.21, 3.22	Send out the Surveys via email and newsletter every 3 months								
3.15	Research the hints on how identify Personas								
3.24, 3.25, 3.28	Research Affinity groups to search for Connectors								
3.29,	Prepare Rewards for Target Readers to encour-								

Task:	Describe Task							
4.17	age engagement every [month][2 months][3 months]							
4.17	Research the types of Rewards I can use							
3.29	Choose from the suggested Rewards							
	Brainstorm with my Team and with my Target Readers other types of Rewards							
	Research Rewards of competing authors							
3.14	Brainstorm with my Team methods to start, maintain and increase the engagement of my Target Readers							
	Research methods used by other authors to engage their readers							
Task 4:	**My Clan of followers:**							
4.5, 4.7, 4.9, 4.15	Prepare my Clan Plan for engaging them and converting readers into Clan members							
	Brainstorm my Clan Plan with my Team							

Task:	Describe Task							
	Ask my readers for suggestions on how to engage my Clan (later on)							
	Research how my Writers Club engages their followers (later on)							
4.11	Ask my Team to ask their friends and relatives to become Clan members							
4.11	Ask my Team to ask their relatives and friends to ask their friends to join my Clan							
4.17, 4.18	Decide on Rewards for Clan members							
4.21	Brainstorm names for your Brand Ambassadors with your Team							
4.23	Prepare Goodies for the diplomatic pouches of your Ambassadors							
4.27	Decide how to measure the Outreach of potential Ambassadors you wish to focus on							
4.28	Ask your Team if they have relatives or friends who might wish to become your Ambassadors							

Task:	Describe Task								
4.28, 4.29	Brainstorm with your Team how to engage and reward Ambassadors								
Task 5:	**My Amazon Blog & Author Blog:**								
5.4, 5.5	Set my Goals for my Author Blog								
5.3	Set up my Author Blog on Blogger								
5	Start My Bloggy Book								
5.12, 5.13	Start collecting Headlines that Hook								
5.13	Ask my Target Readers to send me Headlines that Hook								
5.6, 5.17, 5.25	Study competitors' blogs for ideas re topics, posts, blogging styles etc. and repeat the study every [month][3 months]								
5.20, 5.24	Ask my Team how to make myself interesting for my blog								
5.23	Prepare [number] of Evergreen topics in my Editorial Content Plan								

Task:	Describe Task								
	every [month][2 months][3 months] for use in posts to my Author Blog								
5.25,	Start My Blog Tracker to spy on other blogs for ideas of what works etc.								
5.26	Search Forums every [month][2 months][3 months] for topics for my blog posts								
5.28	Ask my Team and Target Readers for ideas of topics for my blog posts								
5.29	Stock up on public domain pics for my future posts								
5.36	Place my Author Video(s) and Book video(s) on my blog posts								
5.14, 5.15, 5.16, 5.45	Prepare and issue Rewards for comments on my Author Blog								
5.46	Check Google Trends every [month][2 months][3 months] to do some trendwatching and trendriding to find topics for blog posts								

Task:	Describe Task							
5.51	Plan to have 3 future posts (later on 5 posts) on hand at all times							
5.54	Search for other blogs that use Guest Posts							
5.56. 5.58	Do my homework on possible Guest blogs host sites							
5.52	Offer to post as a Guest blogger to [one][two][five] host sites every [month][2 months][3 months]							
5.59	Invite other bloggers to post on my host blog							
5.62	Join Brilliant Bloggers and post some blogs there							
5.67, 5.68	Research Blog tours							
5.69	Prepare my own small blog tour							
5.70	Do homework to see who to invite to join my own Writers Club							
5.67	Do a test blog tour on my Writers Club blogs							
5.27	After 6 months start My Best of Series of blog posts							
5.1	Start my Amazon Author Page							

Task:	Describe Task								
Task 6	**My Facebook Page:**								
6.2	Prepare my Facebook part of my Small Steps Plan								
6.3	Start my Facebook Page								
11.19, 3.22	Prepare a joint contest on Facebook with my Writers Club								
6.9	Join Authors on Facebook								
5.27	Start obeying the 3 Bites Rule for repurposing any message								
6.21	Start an Indie Community Page for Indie writers on Facebook								
6.24	Start my Fan of the Month (FOTM) celebrations								
6.27	Start a series of Facebook polls using polldaddy to gain information and engage readers								
6.28	Research starting a contest on Facebook to engage my readers								
6.31	Run a photo contest on Facebook								

Task:	Describe Task							
6.32	Become a Facebook Groupmeister and start my private Brand Ambassador Group							
6.32	Start my closed Writers Club Group on Facebook							
6.32	Start my open Clan Group on Facebook							
6.32	Brainstorm with my Team about the type of Facebook Group I could form revolving around my book							
6.34	Scan the Internet to find articles on how to engage my readers on Facebook every [month][2 months][3 months]							
6.35	Ask my Clan to scout the Internet to find articles on how to engage my readers on Facebook every [3 months]							
Task 7:	**My Amazon & Kindle Forums:**							
7.4	Check Amazon Communities							
7.4	Check Createspace Community Discussion Boards							

Task:	Describe Task							
7.6	Read rules of Amazon and Kindle communities							
7.7	Search for my initial and second phase Amazon and Kindle communities							
7.9, 7.10	Join [2][4][10] Amazon and Kindle Forums and start participating in conversations							
7.14	Explore the Kindleboards site (including the Writers Cafe, The Book Bazaar & The book Corner)							
7.9, 7.10	Do my homework on Kindleboard							
	Explore the Kindleboard Forum Center Announcements and Tips							
7.5	Select [2][5][10] Kindle Forums and start participating in them							
Task 8:	**Google+**							
8	Draft my Google+ part of my Small Steps Plan							
8	Discuss my Google+ plan with my Team							

Task:	Describe Task						
8.2	Join Google+						
8.1	Bookmark googleplusdaily and dip into it every month						
8.3	Discuss with my Writers Club forming a collaborative Google+ Community						
8.6	Research Influencers using Google+ Ripple						
8.7	Consider with my Team segmenting my Target Readers and forming Google+ Circles for each segment						
8.8	Research Google+ Hangouts and Hangouts on the Air						
8.10	Brainstorm with my Team how to engage my Clan or my Target Readers using Google+ Hangouts and Hangouts on the Air						
8.10	Prepare a Webinar on my Indie Journey (my promotion plans and how I am doing) for broadcast on Google+ Hangout on the Air						
8.12	Research how Book Clubs use Google+ Hangouts and						

Task:	Describe Task								
	Hangouts in the Air								
8.12, 8.13	Launch my own Hangout for my Book Club with my Writers Club								
8.14	Connect with 10 other writers on Google+ every month								
Task 9:	**Pinterest:**								
9.1	Join Pinterest								
9.4	Brainstorm with my Team how best to use Pinterest								
9.5, 9.6, 9.7	Start my boards on Pinterest (including my Clan Board)								
9.11	Cooperate with my Writers Club on a joint set of Pinterest Boards								
9.17	Follow other book bloggers on Pinterest								
Task 10:	**Twitter:**								
10.6	Draft my Twitter part of my Small Steps Plan								

Task:	Describe Task							
10.20	Discuss my Twitter plan with my Team							
10.22	Set my Twitter goals with my Team							
10.1	Join Twitter							
10.24	Start tweeting							
10.27	Invent my own hashtags for Twitter							
10.24, 10.30	Follow selected hashtags							
10.37	Research Twitter Chats and discuss with my Team							
10.37, 10.38	Participate in selected Twitter Chats every [second day][week][other?]							
10.39	Start making friends with Twitter, including my Target Readers							
10.46	Retweet other people's tweets							
10.48	Research Twitter Contests							
10.48	Launch my first Twitter contest targeted at my Target Readers							
10.52	Nurture my Twitter Followers							

Task:	Describe Task								
10.54	Research Twitter Lists								
10.55	Start my own Twitter Lists								
10.61	Research my Twitter Competition								
10.62	Join TweetDeck								
10.62	Prepare delayed tweets for TweetDeck								
10.63	Research GroupTweet and consider using it with my Clan								
Task 11:	**My Email Plan and Newsletter:**								
11.2	Prepare my Email part of my Small Steps Plan and discuss it with my Team								
11.4, 11.5, 11.6	Define my primary and other goals for my Email plan and discuss them with my Team								
11.2	Include in my Editorial Content Plan (ECP) my Themes for my email campaign								
	Subscribe to an email service provider								

Task:	Describe Task							
11.33, 11.34	Learn all the features of my email service provider and discuss with my Team							
11.8	Kick start my email sub-scriber list by inviting friends and family to join							
11.28	Use my Opt-In Form to invite email subscribers to join my Quality Tests Guinea Pigs							
	Write 1 Author Blog post every 3 months describing content of your email campaign and asking for comments from my Target Readers							
11.37	Design 1 quiz every 3 months to gather demo-graphic data (Personas research) from my Target Reader email subscribers							
11.16, 11.55	To reward my email subscribers prepare 1 reward package (a PDF) every 3 months							
11.26	Discuss with my Team methods to improve my click through rates every 3 months							

Task:	Describe Task							
11.18	Prepare 1 Webinar to reward my email subscribers every 6 months							
11.19	Research with my Writers Club best practices for email promotion of my book every 6 months							
11.20	Research every 3 months best practices on email promotion by authors, on Forums and via Google							
11.21	Do one split-level test every 3 months to test headings and content of my email messages							
11.22	Brainstorm contents of my digital Newsletter with my Team							
11.22	Launch my [weekly][bi-weekly][monthly] digital Newsletter							
11.19, 11.23	Research best practices of other Newsletters every 6 months							
11.49, 11.50	Prepare and launch an educational drip marketing plan for my email subscribers							
11.76,	Prepare videos of people reading extracts of my							

Task:	Describe Task							
11.95	book for my email sub-scribers							
11.82	Prepare some evergreen content PDFs for email messages							
11.83	Prepare repurposed material for use with all channels, including email messages							
11.101	Prepare SurveyMonkey surveys for use with email messages to gather demo-graphic date on readers so as to verify and update my Target Reader Personas							
11.106	Prepare a testimonial video from satisfied reader of my book for my email messag-es							
Task 12:	**Listmania:**							
12.1, 12.6	Research Amazon's List-mania							
12.2	Create my lists for List-mania							
12.10	Create cooperative Lists for							

Task:	Describe Task								
	Listmania								
12.15	Tell authors I have listed them in my Listmania lists								
Task 13:	**My Book Reviews:**								
13.21, 13.22	Prepare my Book Review part of my Small Steps Plan covering the 4 kinds of reviews open to me								
13.8	Review Amazon Top Reviewers list								
13.14, 13.25	Prepare my various re-quests for reviews for the experiment with Amazon reviewers								
13.30	Ask other writers who might be a good reviewer of my book								
13.13, 13.24	Start homework on select-ed Amazon Reviewers								
13.26	Ask for reviews from my first panel of targeted Amazon Reviewers								
13.16	Review Amazon Reviewer rules to decide if I should become an Amazon book								

Task:	Describe Task							
	reviewer							
Task 19	Start a cooperative Random Book Review Blog with my Writers Club							
Task 14:	**More Forums:**							
14.1, 14.3	Prepare My Forums part of my Small Steps Plan							
	Brainstorm My Forums plan with my Team							
14.2	Join and contribute to 2 Forums on Amazon							
14.2	Join and contribute to 2 Forums on Kindleboard							
	Do some trendwatching and trendriding on Forums every month at least							
14.1	Join Amazon's Meet our Authors Forum							
	Research how authors have used Amazon's Meet our Authors for self-promotion and use best practices for my Meet our Authors							
	Join conversations (threads) on Amazon's							

Task:	Describe Task								
	Meet our Authors Forum every [3 days][5 days][week]								
14	Select 2 new (non-Amazon and non-Kindle) Forums to participate in every [2 months][3 months], including the following forums: Blog Nation, Goodreads, Shelfari, Onlinebookclub, Digg, Reddit, Stumbleupon, Mobileread forums, Delicious, Squidoo, Anobi Networking, Nexopia Networking, Triberr)								
14.4	Select Book Clubs to join or assist								
Task 15:	**My Clan Team of Advisors:**								
15.3	Ask potential advisors to describe their skill sets								
15.5	Prepare briefing note to potential Clan advisors								
15.6	Prepare quid pro quos for those of the Clan who join your Clan Team of advisors								

Task:	Describe Task								
Task 16:	**YourBookAuthors.com**								
16	Join YourBookAuthors								
16	Form a Guinea Pig Group from members of Your-BookAuthors								
16	Brainstorm with your Team how to use the Guinea Pig Group								
Task 17:	**LinkedIn:**								
17.2	Join LinkedIn								
17.3	Research LinkedIn Groups								
17.9	Join 5 LinkedIn Groups								
17.3	Participate in conversations on LinkedIn								
Task 18:	**Videos, Talk shows & Podcasts:**								

Task:	Describe Task								
18.3	Brainstorm with your Team how best to use videos, talk shows and podcasts in your Small Steps Plan								
18.4	Make your book video								
18.4	Join Book Trailer Central Community								
Task 19:	Working with the Indie Community:								
19	Brainstorm with your Team and Clan Team how best for you to improve the Indie Community								
19	Consider doing the items under the heading TIPS								
Task 20:	Review & Revise:								
20	Review with your Team every element of your Small Steps Plan								
20	Revise the Plan and extend it for a 12 month period								

Task:	Describe Task							

Prepare your *Weekly Engagement Checklist*, and discuss it with your Team, and, later on, your Clan and Ambassadors. Revise it every time you and your Team decide on new or better social media engagement methods.

Every week, go through the *Weekly Engagement Checklist* and carry out the engagement tasks (small steps) in it.

Note: Not every task will be done in each weekly check; some tasks will be done every few weeks.

For starters, your *Weekly Engagement Checklist* will include the following tasks (references are to the Task number and paragraph numbers under each Task in this book):

1. Thank your Team members for their help (Task 1 para 1 or 1.1)

2. Set the Agenda for any Team meeting using *Small Steps to Bigger Book Sales* (1.5)

3. Test with your Team the promotion messages to be sent out this week (1.6)

4. Consider revising or adding to your Editorial Content Plan (1.7)

5. Make any changes to the composition of your Team that are needed (1.8)

6. Check whether any Brand Touches to be made this week are consistent with your Author Brand (2.3)

7. Consider using free samples and free eBooks for your Target Readers (3.4)

8. Consider changing the features of Rebecca Random (3.10)

9. Ask your Target Readers for help in fleshing out your Target Reader Personas (3.12, 3.14, 3.23(r))

10. Check this week's messages against your family of Personas (3.17)

11. Do some role-playing with your Team and your Target Reader Personas (3.18)

12. Talk to your Target Reader Personas (3.19)

13. Consider a Survey of your Target Readers to find your Lost Tribes (3.21)

14. Consider Joint Surveys of readers along with Indie Community members (3.22)

15. Check for Affinity Groups as potential Clan members (3.23(w), 3.24, 3.25)

16. Ask your readers to become Clan members (3.29)

17. Ask Team to think of relatives and friends who could become guinea pig Clan members to kick start the Clan (4.11)

18. Recognize any person who comments or interacts with your Facebook page, blog posts or other messages; and thank them (4.12)

19. Check this week's messages to make sure they meet the three primary motives of social media players (4.13)

20. Join conversations on Twitter, Facebook, forums (4.16)

21. Involve with the Indie Community (4.18(c))

22. Decide how to work with others to design and award Indie Recognition Awards (4.19)

23. Check for new types of rewards to be used to recognize your readers (4.18(e))

24. Follow people on Twitter and explain why (4.18(f)

25. Ask people on Follow Friday to follow those new followers of yours (4.18(g))

26. Include a Quote Gift on your blog post this week (4.18(i))

27. Prepare your Author at Work Peeks for rewards (4.18(j))

28. Ask your Target Readers for input into your next book (4.18(k))

29. Test your Guinea Pigs on items they have agreed to be involved in (4.18(m), 4.18(n))

30. Prepare your Newsletter (4.18(p))

31. Issue your Newsletter (4.18(p))

32. Prepare Checklists are Rewards for your Target Reader Personas (4.18(q))

33. Prepare Interviews with Clan members (4.18(s))

34. Brainstorm with your Team for more WOW in your messages and rewards (4.18(s))

35. Prepare Goodies for the diplomatic pouches of your Ambassadors (4.23)

36. Ask 5 Clan members personally to spread Ripples (4.26)

37. Track social network of potential high-intensity Ripplers using social metrics (4.27)

38. Consider writing new lessons for your Indie Ambassador 101 lesson series (4.28)

39. Cooperate with other Indies in setting up joint Indie Ambassador 101 lessons

40. Roll out new lessons in your Indie Ambassador 101 series (4.28)

41. Check the rewards set out in 4.29 to reward Influencers to see which ones need tending this week (4.29)
42. Ask your Target Readers for UGC (User Generated Content) you can use (4.30)
43. Jot down new ideas in My Bloggy Book (5)
44. Discuss with your Team whether you are meeting your Author Blog goals (5.5)
45. Ask your Target Readers to give you ideas for better headlines for a future blog post (5.12)
46. Add some Headlines that Hook to My Bloggy Book (5.12)
47. Acknowledge the contribution of others to your Blog comments (5.14, 5.16)
48. Follow some commentators on your author blog (5.15)
49. Study the comments on the blogs of some of your competitors to gain hints on what is trending (5.17)
50. Dip into Blogger Stats to check your blogging progress (5.20)
51. Write some Evergreen Posts for future Author Blog posts (5.23)
52. Research 2 other bloggers (5.25)
53. Check forums for ideas for this week's blog posts (5.26)
54. Apply the Three Bites Rule to your blog posts (5.27)
55. Ask your Target Readers for ideas for future blog posts (5.28)
56. Consider what needs to be done with the ideas in 5.33 to 5.51

57. Prepare a blog post for your Guest Blogging & Blog Swap (5.52, 5.53)
58. What steps do you need to do this week to prepare for your future Blog Tour? (5.67)
59. Check if you are using the Facebook tips in 6.5
60. Create an Event for your Facebook (6.6, 6.14)
61. Check how to improve your Facebook presence (6.19)
62. Consider posts in your character Facebook pages (6.20)
63. Consider a contribution to your Indie Community Facebook page (6.21)
64. Prepare your Fan of the Month selection (6.24)
65. Prepare a special Facebook post for your Custom Facebook List (6.26)
66. Consider a poll for your Facebook page (6.27)
67. Consider a contest on Facebook (6.28)
68. Consider fresh entries on your private Facebook Groups for your Writers Club, your Clan and your Ambassadors (6.32)
69. Enter conversations in the Amazon, CreateSpace and Kindle boards (7.3, 7.9, 7.10, 7.12, 7.13, 7.14)
70. Search Amazon Communities for new communities that would fit your outreach messages strategies (7.7)
71. Start a conversation using Google+ Communities (8.1)
72. Prepare a Google+ Hangout for your Team (8.4)
73. Prepare a Google+ Hangout for your Clan (8.4)
74. Prepare a Google+ Hangout for your Ambassadors (8.4)

75. Prepare a Google+ Hangout for your Writers Club (8.4, 8.12)
76. Check the Google+ Ripples of a competitor (8.6)
77. Polish your Google+ Circles (8.7)
78. Prepare for your Google Hangouts on Air event (8.9, 8.10)
79. Post pictures on Pinterest (9.4)
80. Ask your Target Readers to post their pictures on your Pinterest Board (9.7)
81. Post pictures and ask your Target Readers to post their pictures on your Indie Pinterest Board (9.9)
82. Post pictures on your Clan Pinterest Board (9.14)
83. Follow some book bloggers on Pinterest (9.17)
84. Check your Twitter Lists to see if they need revising (10.2)
85. Consider using some of the ways to use Twitter as an author in 10.18 and 10.22
86. Check the Twitter hashtags set out in 10.24 and 10.30
87. Mention a few Clan members on Twitter (10.33)
88. Join and talk in some Twitter Chats for writers (10.37, 10.38)
89. Retweet some of your Clan member tweets (10.46)
90. Check the influence of some of your Clan member Twitter accounts using Tweetgrader (10.49)
91. Check your own Twitter influence using Tweetgrader (10.49)
92. Nurture some of your Twitter followers this week (10.52)

93. Follow some Tweeters who have followed you (10.53(3))
94. Follow on Twitter some bloggers (10.53(4))
95. Ask your Target Readers who you should follow on Twitter (10.53(5))
96. Discuss with your Team setting up a Debate on Twitter and your Blog about some topics in your book (10.53(7))
97. Check whether you are using your Twitter Follower Lists effectively (10.54, 10.56, 10.57)
98. Research the Tweet Clouds of some of your competition and discuss your findings with your Team and send a message to your Target Readers about your findings (10.61)
99. Plan some future Tweets using Tweetdeck (10.62)
100. Bounce your planned weekly Email message(s) off your Team to make sure your goals are clear and are met by the message content (11.4, 11.25)
101. Research other Newsletters for hints for your own Newsletter (11.23)
102. Review with your Team your Email success metrics and take improvement actions if needed (11.26)
103. Review with your Team your Email segmenting efforts to see if they need fine-tuning (11.37)
104. Brainstorm with your Team new kinds of Calls to Action for your Email messages (11.40)
105. Review your Email Drip Marketing Campaign with your Team (11.50)

106. Review your Listmania lists and use of those Lists and update them (12.2)

107. Approach more Amazon Book Reviewers to ask them to review your books (13.13)

108. Ask others to review your books (13.14)

109. Write some reviews for books on Amazon (13.16, 13.17)

110. Search for other non-Amazon book reviewers and ask them to review your books (13.18, 13.19, 13.21)

111. Check for new lists of book reviewers (13.32)

112. Search for new forums for your book genre (14.1)

113. Self-promote yourself and your books on Amazon's Meet Our Authors Forum (14.1)

114. Writes posts for selected Forums set out in Task 14

115. Test some messages with your Guinea Pig Group from YourBookAuthors (Task 16)

116. Nurture your LinkedIn Groups (17.3)

117. Search for new LinkedIn Groups for your to join (17.9)

118. Prepare a Book Video or Author Video or a Podcast (Task 18)

119. Prepare 2 tasks for this week to boost the Indie Community (Task 19)

120. Review and revise your Small Steps Plan (Task 20)

About the Author

Glenn Ashton, who writes interesting books, used to be a banker and a lawyer but had more fun writing novels than wrestling with finance and the law, and so turned his hand to his hobby. Glenn Ashton is the penname of Glenn van Schalkwyk.

He has written several thrillers, a play, and children's books.

His Amazon author site is at:

https://www.amazon.com/author/glennashton

His author blog is at:

http://glennashton.blogspot.com

You can email him about your own journey with your own Small Steps Plan, at:

smallsp@telus.net

www.ingramcontent.com/pod-product-compliance
Lightning Source LLC
Chambersburg PA
CBHW051851170526
45168CB00001B/63